3 DIMENSIONAL WEALTH

A RADICALLY SANE PERSPECTIVE ON WEALTH MANAGEMENT

Monroe M. Diefendorf, Jr.,
and
Robert Sterling Madden

3 Dimensional Wealth™ is a trademark of The Foundation for the Encouragement & Preservation of Family Values, LLC
Certified 3 Dimensional Wealth Practitioner and C3DWP are certification marks of 3 Dimensional Wealth International, LLC

Submit all requests for reprinting to:
Greenleaf Book Group LP
4425 Mopac South, Suite 600
Longhorn Bldg., 3rd Floor
Austin, TX 78735
(512) 891-6100

Published in the United States by
3 Dimensional Wealth Publishing
Locust Valley, NY

Layout by Greenleaf Book Group
Cover design by Greenleaf Book Group
First Edition
Tracking Number: 067979

To laugh often and much, to win the respect of intelligent people and the affection of children, to earn the appreciation of honest critics and endure the betrayal of false friends, to appreciate beauty, to find the best in others, to leave the world a bit better, whether by helping a child, a garden patch, or a redeemed social condition, to know even when one life has breathed easier because you lived, this is to have succeeded.

—Ralph Waldo Emerson

Money is a great treasure that only increases as you give it away.

—Sir Francis Bacon

We make a living by what we get, but we make a life by what we give.

—Winston Churchill

Riches are the least worthy gifts which God can give man. What are they to God's Word, to bodily gifts, such as beauty and health, or to the gifts of the mind, such as understanding, skill, and wisdom? Yet men toil for them day and night, and take no rest. Therefore, God commonly gives riches to foolish people, to whom he gives nothing else.

—Martin Luther

God has given us two hands—one to receive with and the other to give with. We are not cisterns for hoarding! We are channels made for sharing.

—Billy Graham

Life engenders life. Energy creates energy. It is by spending one's self that one becomes rich.

—Sarah Bernhardt

Love the Lord your God with all your heart and with all your soul and with all your mind and love your neighbor as yourself.

—Jesus of Nazareth

CONTENTS

Acknowledgments

MONROE M. DIEFENDORF, JR.: I could not have reached this point in my life without the guidance of God and the values passed on to me by my parents Evelyn and Monroe Diefendorf. A simple "thank you" is inadequate to express my deep appreciation for the love and support of my wife Chris and my children, Ashley, Jennie, Whitney, and Emily. For thirty years I have earned our living, but Chris has made the living worthwhile. I give a special thanks to Greer Kendall, the father of 3 Dimensional Wealth. He is a living example of the 3 Dimensionally Wealthy man, first as a successful financial planner and now as a missionary to Zambia. I am grateful to Peter Reganato, Chris Diefendorf, Evelyn Diefendorf, Martha Diefendorf, and Monroe Diefendorf, Sr., for their patient labors in editing this book. To Mark Carver, PhD, and his lifelong career as a counselor and therapist, who helped create the curriculum for the Certified 3 Dimensional Wealth Practitioner (C3DWP) designation. I trust our efforts will help in shaping the future of the financial planning profession. Finally, to my coauthor Bob Madden for taking this book from its seminal stage to its conclusion. His life lessons and experiences are invaluable to those who earnestly seek harmony and balance in their lives.

ROBERT STERLING MADDEN: My life is a work in progress fueled by a continuing quest for knowledge and a thirst to understand God's will for me. I am a unique creation of God, who is the fount of wisdom, understanding, and love. My personal, financial, and social wealth derive from the gifts and talents He has graciously given to me. It is my responsibility to use them in this way. My deepest thanks go to Cindy, my wife and helpmate for thirty-two years, for broadening my understanding of all three dimensions of wealth. She personifies "walking the talk" by helping those in need first and thinking of herself last. She actually does what others think they should do but usually fall short of doing. I thank my parents Paul and Lena Madden, now deceased, who lived 3 Dimensional Wealth lives. Their core values, beliefs, and attitudes of living life to its fullest, and being committed to God, family, and friends, provided the solid foundation on which I built my life. I would like to thank Roey Diefendorf for turning dreams into realities, for pushing gently to get the book moving, and Peter Reganato for selflessly jumping in to see it to completion. Lastly, I strongly urge my children, Rob and his wife Cheri, Michael, and Alie to consider the concept of 3 Dimensional Wealth as a legacy for their children and grandchildren. The torch has been raised. Willing hands must carry it forward.

Preface

There are many self-help books on the dynamics of wealth building and on strategies that lead to a successful life. By today's standards, success is usually defined by a person's financial wealth or, more specifically, his financial statement. This "balance sheet of life" reflects the assets and liabilities—created or inherited—that a person has, and in some ways it defines the person and his measure of success. The thesis of this book challenges current definitions of wealth and success. Is the person with the most toys the most successful? Is net worth measured by the accumulation of money and "stuff" the hallmark of success? Can a person achieve success solely by acquiring goods or cash? Can someone who accumulates substantial financial assets actually be unsuccessful? Does a robust financial statement truly indicate success? Or is there a better method to assess true success and wealth . . . and their significance in today's materialistic world?

A balance sheet of life becomes more significant when the key words *balance* and *life* are explored and put into practice. A balance sheet is a statement of income and expense characterized by debits and credits. When debits are greater than credits we're in the black, or positive on our balance sheet. But there is a second set of "books" that presents a different kind of balance sheet. Instead of an accounting of income and expense, this balance sheet represents an accounting of one's consumption patterns (inflow) versus giving patterns (outflow). *Inflow* is money or resources accumulated for use in our own interest; *outflow* is money or resources used for the benefit of others or what might be called "matters of significance."

Ironically, in this balance sheet of life, the outflow is of greater significance than the inflow. Here, neither success nor wealth is measured by what is accumulated, but by what is spent or contributed to benefit others. This approach symbolizes a life of significance, which transcends death. It carries success achieved during one's lifetime to future generations.

The purpose of this book is to introduce a radical and inspiring concept to interweave the goals of success, wealth, and significance to increase meaning in life. It will help to redefine success and wealth and depict it in a new balance sheet based on one's personal, financial, and social life. It is the intent of this book to replace preconceived notions of wealth with a broader definition—3 Dimensional Wealth.

I | THE ROAD TO 3 DIMENSIONAL WEALTH

INTRODUCTION

Life's journey begins and ends at a different time and place for each of us. Your starting point is not of your choosing. Though you can choose your ultimate destination and goals, your ending point is unknown. God gives you unique gifts and talents that you can develop and use, ignore, or misuse. However, in large measure, *you* define and control your journey. You determine the roads to be taken to help you achieve your goals.

YOU DEFINE AND CONTROL THE JOURNEY

The journey begins with your understanding of the concept of wealth as it relates to the three dimensions of your life: personal, financial, and social. Personal wealth refers to who you are; financial wealth refers to what you have; and social wealth refers to how you can make a difference. Each dimension by itself can lead to success but not necessarily to significance. Integration of the three wealth dimensions, however, achieves significance.

This new approach to wealth requires you to turn your thinking inside out. It takes you from a wealth-accumulation strategy of save, spend, and give what's left over, to a new strategy of give first, save, and spend what's left over. You enter a new "zone" that has three distinct dimensions, each of which represents a unique part of wealth. During your journey we will help you define your values, attitudes, and beliefs, and clarify your life's vision, mission, and purpose. Ultimately, you will reach your final destination of self-fulfillment with a 3 Dimensional Wealth legacy to pass on to future generations.

WARNING: THE ROAD TO 3 DIMENSIONAL WEALTH HAS POTHOLES

New York has some of the largest and deepest potholes in America. We have experienced their damaging effects as we drive to our daily destinations. They can make even the shortest drive dangerous. "Potholes" may hinder your progress to wealth creation and success can be pockmarked and littered with obstacles and detours. Care must be taken to avoid these dangers. In the journey metaphor that is discussed in chapter 1, we explain how a "map" and a "compass" are essential to successfully reach your destination. In some cases, you must maintain your "road" by making repairs to ensure safe transit. Similarly, you must avoid personal potholes that can seriously impede your journey. Some potholes appear due to poor planning, misinformation, and regretful choices. Other potholes are unavoidable, such as illness, world events, and the unforeseen actions of others. A combined fifty years in financial planning has convinced us that a fresh approach to wealth is necessary to successfully avoid the potholes all of us are sure to face throughout our lives.

WHAT IS WEALTH?

Activate a computer search engine and type in the word *wealth.* A host of subjects appear ranging from personal finance and business to investing and banking, with the words *money* or *finances* as common threads. Wealth is typically defined as a measure of one's financial status. There are those who believe that wealth is associated specifically with money and possessions. While financial assets—money, property, and possessions—are components of wealth, it is important to view wealth in a much broader perspective.

FINAL DESTINATION: 3 DIMENSIONAL WEALTH

First, an understanding of wealth and its relevancy to success is essential. There are those who believe that wealth is evil. Many quote 1 Timothy 6:10, "For the love of money is a root of all kinds of evil." Others believe net worth is a measure of a person's self-worth. They measure in primarily financial terms. In *The American Idea of Success*, Richard Huber observes, "In America, success has meant making money and translating it into status or becoming famous . . . it meant attaining riches or achieving fame . . ." A familiar bumper sticker asserts "The one who dies with the most toys wins," which is a materialistic goal of many. The truth probably lies somewhere in the middle. Financial wealth has value for the right purpose. Without money, commerce becomes cumbersome. In our global society, money lubricates the wheels of commerce. However, in spite of our many years as financial planners, we have arrived at the conclusion that wealth has relatively little to do with money.

WEALTH IN RELATION TO MONEY

When oil executive and financier J. Paul Getty, considered to be one of the richest men in the world in the 1950s, was asked how much money is enough, he replied, "Just a little bit more." Today, this sentiment seems to be the norm. However, those who believe that the accumulation of money is life's ultimate reward have created a pothole that can never be filled. They may try to fill it with possessions, relationships, titles, etc., but the stubborn void usually remains.

Each of the potholes associated with personal, financial, and social wealth takes a toll on the family structure. These potholes include misuse of time or money, health issues, peer pressure, and lack of education. The daily pressures of life must also be considered. More must be accomplished in less time. Not too long ago, snail mail was an adequate means of transmitting written correspondence. Now, those without e-mail are severely handicapped. The tensions of life have tightened. Stresses have increased. Priorities of life are skewed. In many cases, both spouses must work to maintain an "acceptable" standard of living. Marriages are sorely tested, and more than 50 percent end up in the divorce courts. Families disintegrate. On the average, families are together for a mere three out of twenty-one meals per week. Children mature with the influences of their peers and MTV. Millions of Americans are categorized as obese. Family church attendance is down 56 percent from a generation ago. Only 2–3 percent of workers will be financially independent when they retire.

In the social dimension, self-centeredness is rampant in our modern culture. Instant gratification is the goal of many. Moreover, the government, not the individual, is the major source of social programs as indicated by the usage of our tax dollars:

Social Security	38% ($798 billion)
Social Welfare Programs	21% ($441 billion)
National Defense	20% ($420 billion)
Physical, Human, and Community Development	10% ($210 billion)
Interest on National Debt	8% ($168 billion)
Law Enforcement and General Government	3% ($63 billion)

(Source: *2002 IRS 1040 Booklet*)

Our forefathers came to America to provide us with the opportunity to have freedom of choice in seeking personal, financial, and social wealth. The legacy we received from them is endangered. Many have lost sight of the principles our country was founded on. The obsession of "reaching the top" and the desire for status through materialism runs rampant. A new understanding of wealth—a 3 Dimensional understanding—is essential to negotiate life's potholes and roadblocks.

A true perspective of wealth encompasses more than just finances. Unfortunately, the training and education financial planners receive focus on the financial aspects of life. While finances can affect the quality of one's life, without a proper appreciation for the "big picture" and an all-encompassing perspective of one's wealth, life will be less than what God intended it to be.

3 DIMENSIONAL WEALTH IS THE TOTAL MEASUREMENT OF ONE'S LIFE

We have concluded that wealth has three specific components: personal, financial, and social. The total measurement of these three components in one's life is 3 Dimensional Wealth. Your journey to 3 Dimensional Wealth will help define, articulate, and integrate all three aspects of your wealth. By integrating the dimensions of your wealth, that is, shaping and aligning all three dimensions, your final destination will be more satisfying and fulfilling and have lasting significance.

The 3 Dimensional Wealth model is not just a road map that shows you how to avoid the potholes in life, but a methodology designed to change your life from merely survival to one of success and significance. Each aspect of our model begins with a definition of its wealth dimension followed by some truths and misconceptions that often cloud the thinking process for those seeking wealth. As with any sound structure, each "wealth model" is built on a solid foundation and has a strong superstructure to withstand the buffets and tremors of life. Each aspect of the model is important, and conviction is critical to action. The resulting plan maps the journey and maintains the course toward achieving 3 Dimensional Wealth.

1 | A Road Map, a Compass, and a Final Destination

Before a journey is started to an unfamiliar place, it is common practice to consult a map, a two-dimensional illustration covering the area to be traveled that usually includes the starting point and the final destination. The map provides information regarding routes available, the shortest distance to the destination, the most scenic route, and, possibly, the fastest way to get there. Knowing before going is a valuable principle, otherwise, as Yogi Berra observed, "If you don't know where you're going, you'll end up somewhere else."

Travelers who want to record the distance of a trip and route information for future reference will set a vehicle's odometer to zero at the onset of the trip and note the mileage at the end of the trip. They may also highlight their maps to mark the most desirable routes. Travelers may differ as to the routes they will take to a common destination. Some will choose the shortest route and others will choose the most scenic route, but if the maps are used properly, all the travelers will eventually arrive at the same destination.

Just as a road map is used for a traveler's journey, a "life map" is used for an individual's journey through life. This journey involves choices or detours that may steer you away from your intended direction. Following clearly charted roads is essential if you are to avoid pitfalls and achieve your goals. A life map, a representation of your life, will enable you to successfully reach your destination.

Throughout your lifetime, you have been influenced by your parents, family, friends, culture, and environment. These influences are critical to the development of your core values, beliefs, and attitudes, which form the boundaries of your life map. Your convictions dictate how closely you follow the road.

Your life's road map can be depicted in one, two, or three dimensions. A one-dimensional road is straight with no curves, rises, or dips. It is a life with one goal, one destination, and no freedom of choice. It is reminiscent of a worker ant whose sole purpose in life is to build a home for the queen ant and then die. The worker ant does nothing for its own benefit. The one-dimensional road may allow for a short stop along the way, but it will never allow the traveler to reach his final destination. An example might be the individual who pursues a career that is not compatible with his talents but fails to change jobs because he is in a comfort zone. This person is traveling a one-dimensional road.

A two-dimensional road map is analogous to a *Rand McNally Road Atlas* that, in addition to the usual road map features, may include major construction sites, "best of the road" trips, and a list of URLs of sites where travelers may find additional information. The two-dimensional road map for life is a picture of where you are at present, where you want to go (final destination), and stops along the way (goals), all enclosed within the parameters of your core values, beliefs, and attitudes. Many roads will lead you to your final destination; the choices you make determine the road you take. A two-dimensional map can be drawn for your personal, financial, and social goals. When these two-dimensional life maps are integrated and synchronized, you will have created a three-dimensional map. Blending your two dimensional life goals from each of the three dimensions of your wealth will lead you to 3 Dimensional Wealth.

A successful journey begins with a well-devised plan. The plans necessary to embark on life's journey to significance also require advanced preparation. To assist you in reaching your final destination, you will be shown how to create a life map that will lead you to your final destination, which will be determined by you. The life map will be a 3 dimensional representation of the three facets of your life: personal, financial, and social. It is the first tool you need for your journey.

In addition to a map, a compass can be a valuable aid in maintaining proper direction, especially when the road twists and turns. The compass always points to magnetic north and doesn't change unless it is seriously perturbed by external influences.

Bob Madden pays tribute to his father's service in World War II as an infantry officer with the 94th Infantry Division in Europe. Bob's dad carried a silk field map of the combat area in his belt. However, the map was only one part of his safety net. When the map was used with a compass, determining location and direction were greatly facilitated. In addition to his map and compass, the other indispensable part of his "survival kit" was a Bible. This gave him the "road map" and "compass" he needed to navigate through life. As a reminder of his dad's safety net in times of peril, Bob has the map encased in glass along with his dad's well-worn Bible.

While a life map provides a pictorial representation of your life, a compass determines your direction and helps keep you on course. In William Bennett's *The Moral Compass*, his basic assumption is that much of life is a moral and spiritual journey. Your journey is a process that is guided by your moral and spiritual paths. The steps you take and the paths you choose determine your final destination. Likewise, you must plan for your children's life journeys by providing them with moral influences and a sense of direction—a moral compass.

There are two aspects of a compass that parallel your understanding of life, and your moral compass is analogous to these aspects. First, the compass needle must point in a definite direction. If undisturbed, the needle will align with magnetic north. Since the compass is based on a magnet, objects containing iron that are in close proximity to the compass—such as motor vehicles, belt buckles, mineral deposits, power lines, and electric motors—can cause perturbations. On a long trip, an error of a few degrees early on can place you many miles from your intended destination. Therefore, it is imperative that you determine your "north" before beginning your journey. You must ensure that impurities do not cause your compass to indicate a false direction.

Dishonesty is an example of an impurity that can adversely influence your moral compass. Disregard for honesty can have catastrophic consequences. Even a "minor" dishonest act can have a major influence on your path and, ultimately, your final destination. You may not always travel in a northerly direction, but it will always be your reference.

The second aspect of a compass is the plotting of a course relative to "north." This is accomplished after you take inventory to determine where you are in your life and visualizing where you want to be.

This leads us to the third and most important element of the travel kit, your final destination. Your final destination is analogous to your mission statement, or your purpose in life. If you want to remain in place, or mark time, you have no need for a map or a compass. However, if you can visualize your destination and articulate where you want to eventually be, you have planned well.

You Get Nowhere if You "Mark Time" Through Life.

When you take inventory of your current situation and then determine where you would like to be, you must establish a route that will take you to your final destination. Your destination is a product of your vision, or how you hope to express your purpose in life. Your vision must be determined before you establish short-term goals, objectives, and strategies. When you read the road map, you view the roads that you can take as strategies to realize your visions. Goals are the stops made along the way and can be used to measure progress toward your vision.

In summary, life is a journey that requires planning. A life map portrays the terrain to be traversed, delineates alternate routes to your destination, and indicates possible stops along the way. A compass is necessary to check your direction and keep you on course. Lastly, your final destination, or vision statement, provides focus for your journey.

Destinations and visions vary from person to person. Some people have destinations and visions very similar to your own, while others have neither destinations nor visions. Before you begin your journey, it would be helpful to avail yourself of the experience of someone with a destination and a vision similar to your own who has successfully made his journey—especially if he has marked the best possible route and provided you with the best equipment you will need to arrive at your destination. This book offers that experience and assists in determining an appropriate route.

ROAD MAP TO 3 DIMENSIONAL WEALTH

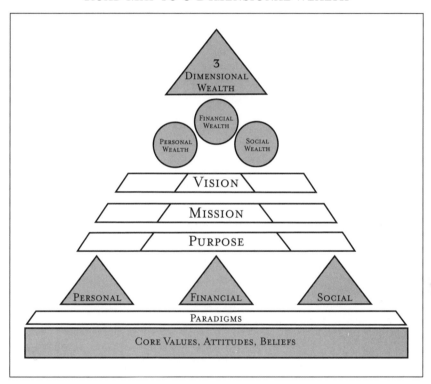

This pictorial life map is presented to help you visualize the main components to achieving 3 Dimensional Wealth.

2 | Calibration

Calibration is the precise adjustment of an instrument for a particular function. It is the fine-tuning that is necessary for optimal performance. Precision military operations, for example, do not just happen by chance. Their accuracy depends on practice drills and calibration. For the military, calibration includes adjusting the bearing and range for a projectile by observing prior attempts at hitting a target. By making modifications based on these observations, the military is ultimately able to hit a desired target repeatedly and with accuracy.

In regard to 3 Dimensional Wealth, calibration refers to aligning your current position with where you hope to be, your destination. It is the vital step in the process that will enable you to get on course, stay on course, and hit your target—or in other words, arrive at your destination.

The purpose of this chapter is to learn how to view the target through a "lens." The lens will help you find direction and aim. It will ensure that you are not haphazardly aiming at your target, but that you are aligning your basic thinking to hit the target. This calibration process will help you to eliminate some of the hesitations and uncertainties in your life and accelerate and enhance your transition from one-dimensional thinking to 3 Dimensional thinking.

The six paradigms listed below were designed to stimulate and redirect your thinking. They are the lens through which you can view life and they will help on your path to discovering 3 Dimensional Wealth.

The Six Paradigms

1. Inwardly focused is out. Outwardly focused is in.

2. Balance sheet accounting is out. Balanced life accounting is in.

3. Spend, save, then give is out. Give, save, then spend is in.

4. Instant gratification is out. Future gratification is in.

5. Ownership is out. Stewardship is in.

6. One-dimensional wealth is out. 3 Dimensional Wealth is in.

As we explore these six paradigms, we hope to challenge you in the way you think. Most people think one dimensionally, because many situations in life require only a one-dimensional thought process. Life and legacy planning, however, requires a new approach. This critical-thinking method will help expand your thought and action processes from one-dimensional to 3 Dimensional.

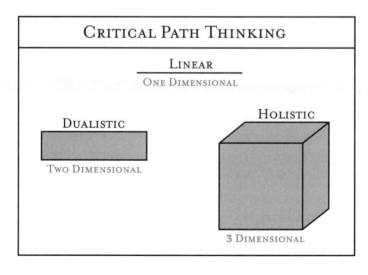

One-dimensional thinking is a relatively simplistic concept that states that something is either black or white, or a shade of grey between the extremes.

Black ——————————————————————✳————————White

The one-dimensional approach to determining a person's wealth is to look at his or her bank account to see where on the rich-poor continuum he or she stands.

Rich ———✳———————————————————————— Poor

One-dimensional thinking looks at a person's life and determines if he or she is growing, stagnant, or somewhere in between.

Growing ——————————————✳———————————— Stagnant

Life is a straight line in a one-dimensional world, and you are some-where on that line. You can create a two-dimensional world by intersect-ing a series of one-dimensional lines. Where these lines intersect will be a "picture" of your two dimensional life. When you shift from considering several aspects of your life independently to seeing how they intersect and complement each other, your life will seem much more substantial. At this point you can expand your way of thinking even further, into 3 Dimen-sional thought.

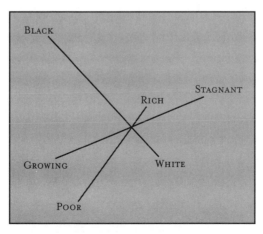

Thinking 3 Dimensionally is our challenge to you to look at life through a different lens—the set of six paradigms. Take a fresh look at your life in terms of the three aspects of wealth and act accordingly. It requires a fresh start to your journey, and always keeping the end, your final destination, in mind. This way of thinking enables you to be open to new ideas and concepts, and challenges you to incorporate them into your life.

---

1. Inwardly Focused Is Out. Outwardly Focused Is In.

Oftentimes life seems to be a paradox. Things just don't seem to be what they actually are. Examples of this are Jesus saying, "The last shall be first," "The weak shall be strong," and "The poor shall be rich." At first glance these paradigms may seem to be oxymorons. Yet, those whose critical thinking has surpassed the one- and two-dimensional stages can appreciate the truth in these statements. When Jesus said, "The last shall be first," he was referring to serving others. When he said, "The weak shall be strong," he was referring not to our strength but to His that empowers. When he said, "The poor shall be rich," he was speaking of humility. Jesus was all about "servant leadership." Doesn't that sound paradoxical? However, our experiences have taught us that the best way to get more out of life is to give more of ourselves.

Monroe Diefendorf, Jr., leads a high school Bible-study group at 6:30 a.m. each Friday. During the year the kids learn the meaning of the expression "stop staring at your belly button" (SSAYBB), which is to focus outward on the world instead of inward, on oneself. Try it yourself. Gaze at your navel. Look hard. Look long. Don't let anything get in the way of a close-up view. How much of the world around you can you see if your focus is centered on your belly button? Your answer will probably be, "Not very much." This inwardly focused, self-centered activity limits the gazer's perspective. It tells you that to get more out of life you need to broaden your view of the world and SSAYBB. Without an outward focus in your life, you will never experience the joy that comes with being others oriented.

Bob Madden has taught his children from an early age that the three most important qualities to cultivate are sharing, caring, and loving. He did this in part through his involvement as a leader of his church youth group. Each of his children witnessed Bob "walk the talk." Now, his twenty-four-year-old daughter Alie, an elementary school teacher, often tells her niece and nephews that they need to share, care, and love. She is passing on what her father gave to her.

These examples illustrate the necessity of an outwardly focused perspective. The first example shows how an inwardly focused view limits options by shutting out the rest of the world, causing a skewed perspective of your life and the lives of others. The second example shows how focusing outward can be rewarding for yourself and for others: not only was Bob able to pass on wisdom to his daughter, but she followed his example and became a model for her niece and nephews.

Our first paradigm sets you in a direction that contradicts the wisdom of the world. The world tells you that to be "successful" it is necessary to ask the question, what's in it for me? This is an inwardly focused, self-centered approach to living. We are asking you to look at the world in a different way. We are asking you to become outwardly focused with an others-centered approach to living. We believe that the question you should be asking is, what's in it for others? Remember, part of your journey is shifting your final destination from success to significance.

2. BALANCE SHEET ACCOUNTING IS OUT. BALANCED LIFE ACCOUNTING IS IN.

When you go to a bank or mortgage company to borrow money for a new car or an addition to your home, it is standard operating procedure for the banker to request a list of your current finances. You begin by writing down all of your tangible assets, for example, your checking account, savings account, investments, brokerage accounts, house, cars, etc. After you have listed your tangible assets, you list all of your debts such as your mortgage and car payments, credit card balances, and student loans. By subtracting your debts from the things you own, you arrive at your net worth. This is your personal financial balance sheet. It may look like this:

MR. & MRS. ONE-DIMENSIONAL WEALTH

STATEMENT OF NET WORTH

	ASSETS	LIABILITIES
CASH	$ 25,000	
INVESTMENTS	$ 125,000	
RESIDENCE	$ 550,000	$ 210,000
401(K) PLAN	$ 238,000	
AUTOMOBILE	$ 25,000	$ 5,000
TOTALS	$ 963,000	$ 215,000

NET WORTH (ASSETS LESS LIABILITIES) . . . . $ 748,000

Preparing a balance sheet of this kind is fine for certain situations, however, it certainly falls short in describing your total wealth. It is an expression of balance sheet accounting only, of your financial assets, and does not account for other assets in your life.

As a way of introducing this idea of balance sheet accounting versus balanced life accounting, each month Monroe Diefendorf invites interested individuals to a 3 Dimensional Wealth Discovery Meeting. Attendees are asked to visualize their wealth in their minds' eyes. This includes their assets and liabilities, their investments, insurance, and last will and testaments. Once they have a mental picture, they are asked if the image related to money—if it had dollar signs "wrapped" around it.

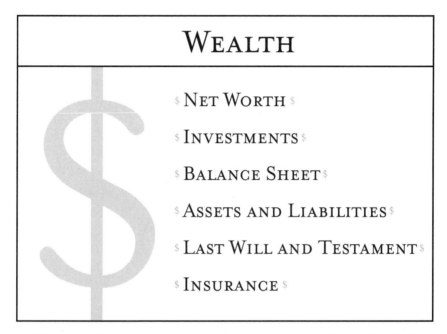

WEALTH

$ NET WORTH $

$ INVESTMENTS $

$ BALANCE SHEET $

$ ASSETS AND LIABILITIES $

$ LAST WILL AND TESTAMENT $

$ INSURANCE $

If you are like most of the attendees, you are conditioned to believe dollar signs signify your wealth. The word *wealth* could be replaced by the word *money*. If you saw the movie *Wall Street*, you might believe that building wealth is about acquiring tangible assets. This is an example of one-dimensional thinking. Unlike your financial balance sheet, your life balance sheet comprises intangible as well as tangible assets.

What does this mean? Tangible assets are measured in dollars and the goods and services those dollars enable you to buy; intangible assets are measured in terms of your heart, soul, and mind. Intangible assets include wisdom, understanding, knowledge, passions, values, convictions, beliefs, and life experiences. The mistakes made and lessons learned, the failures suffered and successes achieved are examples of immeasurable assets. If you were a corporation, goodwill might appear on your balance sheet as an intangible asset. As an individual, the value of these intangible assets can be worth more than anything you could buy with money. In fact, the value of your tangible assets might be significantly lessened if it were not for your intangible assets. For example, knowledge, wisdom, experiences, and friendships all might help you make more informed choices, thus adding to your net worth. Tangible and intangible assets are interrelated and a preoccupation with only one asset type makes it impossible to lead a 3 Dimensionally Wealthy life.

WEALTH COMES IN THREE DIMENSIONS: PERSONAL, FINANCIAL, AND SOCIAL

Our true wealth has relatively little to do with money. We must broaden our concept of wealth beyond our financial balance sheet (net worth) to include our self-worth and our selfless worth. Balanced life accounting takes wealth to another dimension by incorporating our intangible assets. We need to redefine wealth with a balanced life! Rather than ask, what is my net worth? you should ask, what difference have I made?

ANALYZING THE BALANCE SHEET OF LIFE

TANGIBLE ASSETS (MONEY)	$$$$$$$$$
INTANGIBLE ASSETS	
OF THE HEART–PASSIONS AND VALUES	?
OF THE SOUL–CONVICTIONS AND BELIEFS	?
OF THE MIND–WISDOM AND KNOWLEDGE	?
OF A LIFE LIVED–	
MISTAKES MADE AND LESSONS LEARNED	?
FAILURES SUFFERED AND SUCCESSES ACHIEVED	?
NET WORTH*	$?$?$?$?$
*WHAT DIFFERENCE HAVE I MADE?	

---

3. SPEND, SAVE, THEN GIVE IS OUT. GIVE, SAVE, THEN SPEND IS IN.

Madison Avenue advertising encourages us to pursue a lifestyle in which if we want something, we should buy it—*now*! Spend is the order of the day. What remains is ours to "keep." The fact is that most of us don't keep what remains. Financial planners or consultants on the other hand tell us that to become financially independent we must pay ourselves first. For them, saving is the order of the day. The remainder can be spent. In either case, if we choose, the remaining part of our discretionary income can be used for charitable or socially responsible contributions.

As we look through the lens at 3 Dimensional Wealth we see a very different order to our priorities. In lieu of spending or saving first, the paradigm suggests that giving first is the order of the day. Giving means contributing to a cause or person who is important to you. "Paying" yourself is the next priority. By that we mean putting money away for your financial future before you spend it trying to maintain your current standard of living. After giving first and paying yourself second, what remains is yours to spend. Madison Avenue and financial planners might consider gifting as "spending." Our paradigm, however, suggests that purposeful gifting is investing—not spending—in matters of significance, and the returns can be "out of this world."

What I Kept, I Lost. What I Spent, I Had. What I Gave, I Have.
—Persian proverb

As we all know, water exists in three different and distinct states. The chemical composition is the same whether it is steam, liquid, or ice. The same is true with wealth. It comes in three different and distinct states: personal, financial, and social. It is only when we begin to view wealth in its three dimensions—or states—that we can understand wealth in its totality. We must come to understand that a transfer of capital as a gift from our personal financial statement to a charitable trust is not a loss of assets. It is the same asset in a different state. A transfer of capital from one's personal financial statement to pay for a family vacation is not a reduction of one's assets but a transfer from the money bank to the memory bank. Just as with H_2O, the molecules are not lost in a conversion from one state to another.

Giving need not only be in dollars. It can be the volunteering of your time. Remember, time is money because it is simply wealth in another form. We will be discussing more of 3 Dimensional gifting in section III.

4. Instant Gratification Is Out.
Future Gratification Is In.

In this "me" generation, we are led to believe that the "now" is all-important. You want it? Charge it—even if you can't afford the price tag! But where does this lead us? Prior generations set sail to new lands to make a better life for themselves and those who would follow. The legacy they left is the United States of America. Our founding fathers sacrificed greatly so that we might have a better tomorrow. Without the same forward-looking perspective on life, our future generations will suffer the consequences.

The concept of "future gratification" accentuates an important point. Preservation of our values, beliefs, and attitudes are dependent upon how we address them today. A Greek proverb states it this way: "A society grows great when the old men plant trees whose shade they shall never sit under." This is a sacrifice made on the behalf of others. Jesus Christ is the ultimate example of future gratification. He gave his life so that we might live. What must we do today in the here and now to provide for a better tomorrow? Your personal journey will determine the answer. Your decisions today will impact your family and future generations.

What would your retirement income be at age sixty-five if you were not currently saving in your 401(k) plan today? How long would it take to accumulate the resources necessary to buy your home with cash rather than attaining the funds from your banker today? As financial planners we recommend never letting the liability outlast the asset. This means that if you want something today and need to borrow the money to get it, don't let the repayment of the debt extend beyond the life of the asset. The classic case is the individual who takes out a home equity loan to buy a used car that has a five-year life span and begins a payment schedule that will last fifteen years. This is a surefire way to become financially destitute. Remember, there is a price tag for everything. The price tag for getting something now might cost you more in the future.

5. Ownership Is Out. Stewardship Is In.

What does it mean to own something? Does it mean simply that we have possession of or the title to an asset? Does it mean that we must also accept the responsibility to care for and maintain that asset? When we go to the bank to obtain a mortgage to purchase our home, who is it who *really* owns the home, you or the bank? The underlying truth is that ownership is a matter of perspective.

Remember the adage "Is the glass half empty or half full?" Of course, the answer is also a matter of perspective. The same is true with how you look at the three dimensions of your wealth. Do you really own your wealth or are you simply managing what has been entrusted to you? As you search for the answer to this question, identifying the location of "north" on your compass will govern your perspective. By following this perspective, it will become evident that stewardship provides for a less encumbered journey.

"He who dies with the most toys wins" is a modern saying that suggests a way of life that concentrates on the importance of money for selfish purposes. Even people who give generously can be caught up in this drive for self-importance or power. On the contrary, stewardship is your responsibility to properly manage everything that God has entrusted to your care. There are major differences in ownership and stewardship of your wealth. Let's consider some of the components that make these "ships" so different.

3 DIMENSIONAL WEALTH:
A MATTER OF PERSPECTIVE

	STEWARDSHIP vs.	OWNERSHIP
SOURCE OF GOALS	GOD	SELF
TYPE OF GOALS	ETERNAL GRATIFICATION	IMMEDIATE GRATIFICATION
MATERIAL THINGS	TAKEN LIGHTLY	POSSESSIONS IMPORTANT
RELATIONSHIP TO MONEY	STEWARDS	POSSESSORS
ACCUMULATION GOALS	SPECIFIC NEEDS	ACCUMULATE FOR EXCESS
VISION	SEE THE UNSEEN	SEE THE NOW
EMOTIONAL STATUS	FREE FROM ANXIETY	CONCERN FOR MONEY
PRIORITIES	1. GIVING	1. SPENDING
	2. SAVING	2. SAVING
	3. SPENDING	3. GIVING

Stewardship recognizes that God owns it all. We are responsible for the care of *His* assets. We are here on earth only for a short time. Eternal goals, therefore, are truly the long-term goals that must be considered for long-range planning. On the other hand, material "stuff" has a limited duration, and, therefore, should be taken lightly. This approach frees you from the anxiety that comes with "needing" to accumulate bigger, better, and more expensive things and alleviates the emotional attachments you develop to these material objects.

Short-term planning accumulates treasures on Earth. The accumulation of multiple homes or, on a smaller scale, the desire to build an expansive wardrobe are examples of short-term planning. Stewardship, on the other hand, helps give clarity to wants versus needs. Stewardship provides you with the ability to have a perspective from above and to see the needs of both you and your neighbors.

Long-term (eternal) planning lays up treasures in Heaven. Not only does it change your perspective, but it changes your desires. An eternal perspective means considering the future and acting in an appropriate manner by pondering the legacy you leave. It means making plans for those who survive our natural lives. Stewardship will lead a mature individual to a responsible approach to passing on his personal, financial, and social legacy.

One-dimensional financial planners look only at financial wealth and transferring the ownership of one's assets. Managers of 3 Dimensional Wealth understand stewardship and consider the totality of your wealth when planning your journey. Keep in mind, 3 Dimensional Wealth is a combination of short-range planning for Earth, long-range planning for Heaven, and legacy planning for the generations to come.

Stewardship versus ownership: on which "ship" will you embark?

---

6. ONE DIMENSIONAL WEALTH IS OUT. 3 DIMENSIONAL WEALTH IS IN.

Wealth in its totality comprises your personal wealth, your financial wealth, and your social wealth, each of which competes daily for your time. Briefly, your personal wealth is who you are, your financial wealth is what you possess, and your social wealth is how you make a difference.

Calibration uses a lens to view your wealth in all three dimensions. It is the method that helps synchronize and harmonize the three dimensions of your wealth, and leads to your life's fulfillment. Each dimension of your wealth is discussed individually in later chapters.

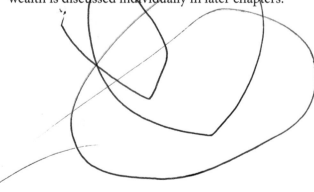

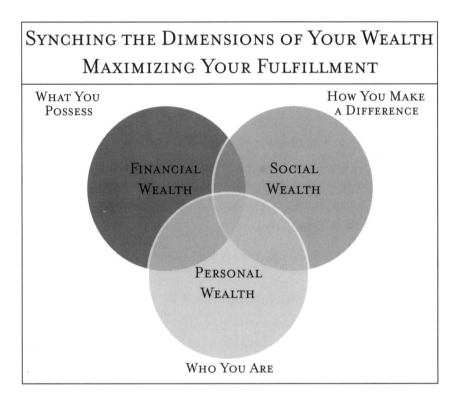

Synching the Dimensions of Your Wealth
Maximizing Your Fulfillment

What You Possess

How You Make a Difference

Financial Wealth

Social Wealth

Personal Wealth

Who You Are

Integrating 3 Dimensional Wealth into your life requires a fresh approach to who you are now and who you hope to become. It may require radical changes that conflict with modern day culture, but total wealth planning will allow you to take control of your life.

What does 3 Dimensional Wealth look like? It is outwardly focused. It uses balanced life accounting. It makes giving (investing in others) your main priority. It understands stewardship. It is a life journey with a predetermined destination. It is a structure built on your core values, attitudes, and beliefs with your purpose, vision, and mission in mind. It will be built to last. And finally, it will be completed by a master architect—you.

3 | BUILT TO LAST

The Great Pyramid of Giza, the most visited of Egypt's pyramids, is the only survivor of the Seven Wonders of the Ancient World. Situated ten miles southwest of Cairo, the Great Pyramid was placed in what was thought to be the exact center of the world. Accidentally or by design, lines drawn through the north-south and east-west axes of the Pyramid equally divide the Earth's terrain. The architect of the Great Pyramid knew where true north was, as the entrance to the Pyramid is oriented in that direction. Therefore, each side is oriented with one of the cardinal points of a compass: north, south, east, or west. The capstone, or the top piece, of the pyramid, is the structure's zenith; all sides of the pyramid converge at the capstone. It is the only stone that covers all corners, unifying the structure.

The ancient Greeks also were known for their architecture. At first glance, it may not be apparent that the buildings of today bear any great resemblance to the glorious temples of ancient Greece, but one can certainly see how we have used their universal building principles to create structures designed to last. In New Hampshire, some of these techniques, such as utilizing post and lintel construction, are used to build barns.

Briefly, here's how it works: A foundation is critical to any structure. Foundations can be bedrock, block, or a slab of concrete. Whatever is used, it is the foundation on which the structure is to be built. A frame called a *sill* rests on the foundation. Pillars, the main upright supports, are attached to the sill, spaced at regular intervals. They are protected from splitting at the top by a block of wood called a *cap*. The lintel, the upper duplicate of the sill, rests on the caps and supports the roof. Triangular frames, or trusses, also support the roof. Three sets of beams run lengthwise and tie the building together; much like the capstone of the Great Pyramid.

These structural features are analogous to our own terms:

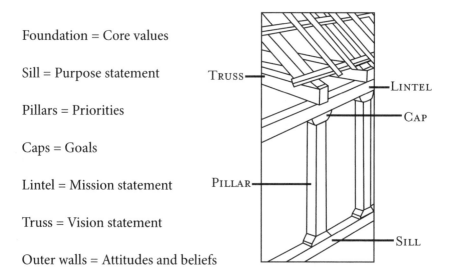

Foundation = Core values

Sill = Purpose statement

Pillars = Priorities

Caps = Goals

Lintel = Mission statement

Truss = Vision statement

Outer walls = Attitudes and beliefs

Structure = 3 Dimensional Wealth

All buildings require a foundation on which the rest of the structure can be erected. A foundation roots a structure in the earth and provides essential support for the rest of the construction. A building's foundation can be considered analogous to your own base structure: your core values. Core values are the bedrock of your being, the foundation on which your life is built. Core values determine how each dimension of your wealth will be constructed.

What do we mean by *core values*? The *core* refers to the part around which everything is formed, the center—or the heart—of an issue. *Values* are a combination of the standards and the ideals that we rely on to make our decisions. Values are the moral compass and common ground by which we judge our actions with respect to our ideals. Values are passed on to us by our families, friends, church, community, school, and culture and are often inspired by God. Values are crucial in determining our behavior, defining us as individuals, setting our priorities, and developing virtue. Core values are the primary building blocks for your life. Together, they represent the framework that allows you to meet the challenge of ethical issues and to resolve them. They allow you to overcome adverse peer pressure and other outside influences. Core values instill confidence and anchor your resolve in the most difficult situations. They unify the foundations on which your decisions are based and are indispensable to achieving a life of significance.

You must articulate, or define, your core values and then communicate them through your actions. According to Alexander Hamilton, "Those who stand for nothing may fall for anything." To build 3 Dimensional Wealth, you must stand for something. This "something" will form the basis for all of your decisions and should represent the ideals and standards central to who you are.

In ancient Greece, Socrates' chief concerns were the perfection of the individual human character and the achievement of moral excellence. Moral values, for Socrates, did not derive from God, as they did for the Hebrews. They were attained when the individual, through rational reflection, created a guiding and ruling agency of the soul. Character was shaped by examining one's life, and, through this critical self-examination, discovering the ethical life through reason. According to Socrates, the unexamined life is not worthy of a human being.

In the same way that core values were important in the ancient world, they remain important today. For example, in today's world, core values are personified by our military organizations. Each of the services predicates its vision and mission statement on core values that are instilled into each armed service member. For the Navy and the Marine Corps, the core values are honor, courage, and commitment. The Army identifies seven core values: duty, integrity, loyalty, selfless service, honor, courage, and respect. The other services have similar core values.

The Bible tells of a man who built his house on sand and another who built his house on rock. When the floods came, the house built on sand washed away while the house built on rock stood firm. The type of foundation determined the survival of the house. Similarly, the strength of your foundation will determine the durability of your structure.

Core values are the foundation of your "life house" that allows it to stand firm when it is buffeted by the trials of life. Do you know your core values? Do they define your character? To determine your core values, you must reflect on your life, which requires a deep, honest assessment of your character. The following list of values is intended to aid in your selection of building blocks for your foundation:

Honesty	Integrity	Courtesy	Kindness
Cheerfulness	Reverence	Bravery	Thrift
Humor	Persistence	Passion	Loyalty
Excellence	Humility	Honor	Self-Control
Patience	Faithfulness	Love	Joy
Peace	Goodness	Gentleness	Respect
Tradition	Courage	Patriotism	Valor
Teamwork	Concern	Selflessness	Dignity
Competence	Service	Obedience	Responsibility
Self-Respect	Justice	Openness	Commitment

As is evident from the list, core values are components of character. Character may be defined as what you do when no one is around. It may manifest itself when the honor code requires a closed-book policy when a take-home exam is given to a student. Character is what you know to be true of yourself. It should not be confused with reputation, which is what others think about you. Reputation is precious, but character is priceless. Without core values to guide you, or if you have unclear values, your character lacks definition.

Complete the following statement using the list of core values above as an aide. Include any values that are important to you that are not listed.

THE MOST IMPORTANT VALUES THAT WILL GUIDE ME IN ALL
FUTURE DECISIONS ARE

_____   _____

_____   _____

_____   _____

_____   _____

All three aspects of wealth—personal, financial, and social—should be built on this foundation of core values. Without a solid, well-constructed foundation, your life house may become unstable and be swept away during the next rainy season.

SUMMARY

Let's review what you have learned. First, a road map portrays the territory in which you intend to travel (life). It also defines the boundaries (core values, beliefs, and attitudes) of that territory. There may be intermediate stops along the way (goals) and these will also appear on the road map. A compass (your moral guide) provides direction to your final destination (life of significance). It also gives you a bearing (right way) by which you can choose your course (freedom of choice). Next, you learned that you must realign your thinking to allow you to understand and accept the way all the pieces fit together. There are six paradigms crucial to this realignment:

1. Inwardly focused is out. Outwardly focused is in.
2. Balance sheet accounting is out. Balanced life accounting is in.
3. Spend, save, then give is out. Give, save, then spend is in.
4. Instant gratification is out. Future gratification is in.
5. Ownership is out. Stewardship is in.
6. One-dimensional wealth is out. 3 Dimensional Wealth is in.

The synergism of the three dimensions of wealth, with the application of the six paradigms, leads to 3 Dimensional Wealth and a life of significance, which is your final destination. Your thinking must be aligned, or calibrated, in such a way that you can understand and accept how all the pieces will fit together.

II

THE SEVEN STEPS TO
3 DIMENSIONAL WEALTH

INTRODUCTION

As you begin your journey into 3 Dimensional Wealth, you will outline seven steps that are critical in navigating through life. Your seven steps include (1) defining core values, (2) taking inventory, (3) taking aim, (4) taking shape, (5) creating your purpose statement, (6) creating your vision statement, and (7) creating your mission statement. Following these steps is necessary to creating a life map. Without a map and a moral compass to give you direction, you may find yourself wandering aimlessly.

Identifying core values sets the foundation for all future steps. These core values are the same for each wealth dimension. It is the only step that is identical for all three aspects. You then begin your process of taking inventory, taking aim, and taking shape. This is followed by the creation of your purpose, vision, and mission statements. The purpose statement is an introspective look at your life and defines what you are here to accomplish. The vision statement looks into the future and gives you a glimpse of what you hope the future will become. Your mission statement is the description of how you are to actually put into action your strategies to fulfill your purpose.

The chapters in this section will teach you how to "take inventory," "take aim," and "take shape" for each dimension of your total wealth. This approach to life differs from the all-too-often "ready, fire, aim" philosophy that permeates our society. With the ready, fire, aim approach, the decision-making process can often be short-circuited by a desire for instant gratification. Initially, you may feel good about a short-term outcome, but often you become discontented or even guilty about your actions when you see the results of your choices. This can lead to frustration with the decision-making process. A change to a "ready, aim, fire" approach through the process of taking inventory, taking aim, and taking shape will provide satisfying results to decision-making.

A worksheet is provided at the end of chapter 8 in order to personalize your steps.

4 | THREE SHORT STORIES ABOUT YOURSELF

Yogi Berra once said, "You can observe a lot just by watching." Rarely do we "watch" ourselves. You could probably describe your spouse, other family members, or a friend more accurately than you could describe yourself. In this chapter, you will try to observe your own behavior by coming up with three stories about yourself. Each story will relate to a different dimension of your wealth.

PERSONAL WEALTH

When discussing personal wealth, address it from the aspect of who you are and why you exist. Taking inventory of yourself will ultimately help you define who you want to be. Purpose, or taking aim, is a reason for being and must be revealed, otherwise you will continue to "fire before aiming." Part of the discovery process is to explore your strengths and weaknesses, to reflect on past experiences, and to visualize the future. Your personal wealth takes shape when you address who you are physically, intellectually, spiritually, socially, professionally, and how you view relationships. The result of this discovery process can be love, joy, peace, patience, kindness, goodness, faithfulness, gentleness, and self-control. Vision and purpose statements produce a clear mind and reinforce a sense of meaning. As you discover yourself, a definition of who you are and why you exist will emerge.

The first step in understanding your personal wealth is to ask, "Who is (your name)?" In about 250 words, describe who you are and *why* you exist? Be sure to include your strengths *and* weaknesses.

FINANCIAL WEALTH

When we discuss financial wealth, we are addressing the "stuff you own" side of your life. Financial wealth is not only a statement of the financial assets that you own, but it is also about the values most important to you. The way you save or invest your money is reflected in your financial wealth statement. The way you *spend* your money is a reflection of who you are and what is important to you. Look at your checkbook and credit card statements. Both are statements of your lifestyle. When it comes to financial wealth, there are many individuals who fire before aiming. In today's world, debt is a form of bondage that is indicative of firing before aiming. Certainly there are situations that have placed people in difficult financial situations through no fault of their own, but more often than not they place themselves in such situations.

The first step of the financial-planning process is to take inventory, which means analyzing your current situation. The second step is to take aim, which requires formulating your goals and objectives. The third step is to take shape, which means devising a strategy that will allow you to get where you want to be.

It is not how much money you own or make, but what you do with it that matters. There are basically three actions you can take with your money: spend it, save or invest it, or give it away. What order of money utilization do you suspect will bring you the greatest success?

The first step in understanding your financial wealth is to ask, "How does (your name) spend money?" In about 250 words, describe *how* you spend your money. What are your greatest financial successes and your greatest financial failures? What's important about money?

SOCIAL WEALTH

When you discuss social wealth, you are addressing how your wealth can make a difference. Social wealth involves identifying an individual in need and/or a community's needs, determining what you can do to answer those needs, and then taking action. It is a statement of your "heart style." Partially it is about giving your money, but it is also involves giving of your time and energy. It is about giving away things that are "easy" to let go of, as well as giving sacrificially for the benefit of others. Social wealth is an expression of an outwardly focused approach to life.

As in the personal and financial wealth exercises, the first step of the social planning process is to take inventory. You will then need to take aim, which will allow you to determine the best utilization of your limited resources. Taking aim will enable you to prioritize your goals and objectives for maximum efficiency. Finally, you will need to take shape by developing strategies that will help you realize your goals and hit your target.

The first step in understanding your social wealth is to ask, "How does (your name) give?" In about 250 words, describe to whom you give of your time, talents, and money; what the greatest rewards are that you have received as a result of your gifting; and the greatest shortcomings in your gifting efforts.

TAKING YOUR FIRST STEP

The reason you wrote these short stories is to stimulate your thinking and start the process of self-discovery. This is an important step in taking inventory. Use the stories as a reference tool as you progress through chapters 5–7.

Viewed through the lens of the six paradigms, you should notice the synergism among your personal wealth, financial wealth, and social wealth. The three dimensions of your wealth compete for the twenty-four hours in each day you are given. They can either work against each other or they can work with each other. The outcome is up to you. The following three chapters will allow you to define and articulate your 3 Dimensional Wealth to improve your chances of success and significance.

5 | PERSONAL WEALTH

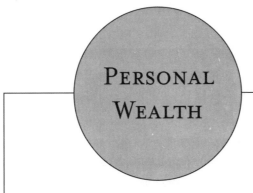

PERSONAL WEALTH

- TAKING INVENTORY—WHO ARE YOU NOW?

- TAKING AIM—WHO DO YOU WANT TO BE?

- TAKING SHAPE—WHAT MUST YOU DO TO BECOME WHO YOU WANT TO BE?

WHO ARE YOU?

Personal wealth is all about who you are. However, understanding yourself is not as easy as you might think. We all have blind spots and see distorted images of ourselves when we look in the mirror. Sometimes you see what you want to see and other times you see something else entirely, including what you don't want to see. But the fact remains, you exist and you must deal with who you are. To understand and maximize your personal wealth, you need to complete a self-discovery process.

There are three major steps you must take in the discovery process of understanding personal wealth. These steps are similar to what you will go through when you unveil the other two dimensions. These three steps are part of your road map that will lead you to 3 Dimensional Wealth.

Taking inventory: Who are you now? (Current situation)

Taking aim: Who do you want to be? (Goals)

Taking shape: What must you do to become who you want to be? (Strategies)

Time passes swiftly. If you are diligent in defining your personal goals (taking aim) and focused in changing your ways (taking shape), then you will have every chance to become all you desire to be. Fortunately, you do have a choice, and it is your responsibility to carpe diem, i.e., seize the day, or as NASA says, "Do it. Do it right. Do it right now." The key is recognizing that you should have begun your journey "yesterday."

Since you cannot change the past, you must begin your journey today. It is also important to keep in mind that personal success is not necessarily all about you. You should refer to your list of core values and the six paradigms that guided the recalibration of your thinking. It will be important to keep these in mind as you take aim and take shape. By looking through your newly acquired 3 Dimensional lens you will learn more as you create your life map and build your life structure.

To begin your journey to personal wealth, answer the following questions: Why do you exist? Where did you come from? What happens when you die? Don't worry if you can't answer these questions immediately; philosophers have spent lifetimes searching for the answers. However, your journey to personal wealth will not be complete until you have answered to your own satisfaction why God has placed you on Earth. Your road map will help you answer some of these questions, and your answers will be the driving force behind your personal wealth statement. You must not only identify the special gifts and talents that God has given you, but you must also take your responsibility of stewardship seriously and put those talents and gifts to proper use. Kevin McCarthy, author of *The On-Purpose Person*, puts it in simple terms: "You are on-purpose when your heart, head, and hands are aligned and integrated with the highest values."

God has a purpose for your life. Ephesians 2:10 states, "For we are God's workmanship, created in Christ Jesus to do good works, which God prepared in advance for us to do." You have been given talents and strengths unique to you. It is your journey to discover what God's purpose for you is. Too many creations of God are missing the journey. They never discover their niche, and they wander without purpose, never being able to say why they exist. They never achieve personal wealth.

There are three basic levels of consciousness in which people live their lives of personal wealth. First, there is the personal survival level. An example of this type of living is people who work all week to get to the weekend and party all weekend so they can face the workweek. Life may seem exciting at times, but there is no sense of fulfillment. Instant gratification typifies survival-level participants.

Second, there is the personal success level. These people drive a luxury car, for instance, have a comfortable house and a vacation home, and a lifestyle to accompany these things. By the world's standards, these people have it made; life is pretty good. But even among financially successful people, many ask, if I really am successful, why don't I feel good about myself? Why am I not fulfilled? The answer is that material success by itself does not completely meet the needs of their personal wealth structure. There are chasms that need to be filled and they can't be filled with money and possessions.

The third level, personal significance, answers the question, why do I exist? Your journey is not intended to lead you to a life of survival or success, but to a life of significance. Your existence has a purpose, and your life matters. Personal significance recognizes the special talents God has given you. Whether it be music, athletic ability, a caring spirit, whatever your special calling, it is the acknowledgment and purposefulness that create this personal wealth. You arrive at a life of significance by following the road map, starting with the core values that shape your attitudes and beliefs. By being faithful stewards of the talents and gifts you have been given, you can move in a positive direction toward personal wealth.

What is exciting about the personal wealth dimension is that, relative to the other dimensions, you have the greatest control over it. *You* decide the parameters associated with the significance of your contributions to life. You are in charge of the evaluation team that grades you at the end of the day. Personal wealth is never the same for two individuals because we are all unique creatures of God. You must discover your uniqueness through your journey.

PILLARS OF IMPORTANCE

Personal wealth is wealth that requires you to take steps to achieve it. It requires a responsible nature and a dedication to personal growth in the areas that you deem important. To get started, you must identify the "pillars of importance" in your life. A thoughtful and honest evaluation of who you are now and what is important to you is essential. How do you do that? We will help you through the process. Although we have not provided an all-inclusive list of areas you might deem important in your life, the following is a list of some possibilities:

Physical	Intellectual	Social	Professional
Health	Mental	Family	Career
Spiritual	Educational	Relationships	Wisdom
Special talent	Time management		

As an example, consider "relationships" as a pillar of importance in your life. It includes your relationships with family and friends. You want to have solid, honest relationships with family and friends, recognizing that this would certainly be a step toward self-fulfillment in your life.

A second pillar of importance could be your "spiritual" walk. We believe this is an integral part of understanding God's purpose for our lives. "Physical" and "health" pillars may also be important in defining your personal wealth. Your physical stature and your physical health will affect you both mentally and physically. A sound mind and body are critical to becoming personally wealthy. Now list your pillars of importance.

STEP 1: IDENTIFYING THE PILLARS OF IMPORTANCE

_____   _____   _____

_____   _____

Having identified the pillars that are key to your personal wealth, now be honest with yourself: are you really committed to this process? You cannot honestly say that health is an important pillar unless you are committed to maintaining good health as an important aspect of your life. For you to take this exercise seriously, you must agree to the following life commitments:

A desire for personal growth
A contribution to those around you (more on this later)
A discipline that will keep you on track
A willingness to make sacrifice today for a greater tomorrow
A system to monitor results and report progress
An attitude that is willing to risk and willing to fail

STEP 2: TAKING INVENTORY

Taking inventory answers the question, who am I? If you ask that question in terms of each of the pillars you have selected, you could come up with a near accurate portrayal of who you are. One way of doing this is to identify your strengths and weaknesses for each of the pillars of importance. For example, in the area of "physical," make a list of your traits, and list them under "strengths," "neutral," or "weaknesses." Some neutral areas might be your height and weight, yet if you felt that these were neutral areas that could be improved on you might consider them weaknesses. Even your strengths might be improved; in fact, it is highly likely you will improve on your strengths if you are committed to personal growth and are willing to make some sacrifices. Be realistic. This is meant to help you determine the possibilities and limitations in your future.

Pillars	Strengths	Neutral	Weaknesses
1.			
2.			
3.			
4.			
5.			

Step 3: Taking Aim

If you were to sit back, close your eyes, and visualize in your mind's eye the person you would like to be, what would you see? Visualization allows you to "see" the "who" you want to be. For example, while putting, many low-handicap golfers can actually see the ball going into the cup before they even touch the ball with a club. Their focus on the desired outcome allows these golfers to consistently achieve success. This is no different for you as you take aim at each of the pillars of importance that you have created. To take aim, you must identify a target. If you could wave a wand to create a successful person within each pillar of importance, who would you see in the near and distant future? Taking aim is about visualizing the future as it could be. The best way to predict the future is to create it.

Using an example of establishing goals within the "physical" pillar, it may be your desire to return to the same weight that you were when you graduated from college. Or a lifelong dream may be to run the New York Marathon. It is important that each goal be specific with vivid details so that it can be measured for success. Don't be afraid to dream big dreams. As Bob Moaward, CEO of Edge Learning Institute, said, "Most people don't aim too high and miss. They aim too low and hit."

PILLARS	SHORT-TERM GOALS	LONG-TERM GOALS
1.		
2.		
3.		
4.		
5.		

STEP 4: TAKING SHAPE

This exercise requires you to establish priorities and devise strategies to reach your goals. You evaluate the importance of each item in relation to the others. Remember, with only twenty-four hours in a day, it is imperative to prioritize your pillars according to their significance to you. As each of these pillars compete for its rank, you must ultimately find the "winner," or as Jack Palance said in the movie *Cityslickers,* "the one thing." This one thing should be addressed first to achieve maximum personal satisfaction and help you become an "on-purpose person."

PILLARS	STRATEGIES
1.	
2.	
3.	
4.	
5.	

Now that you have worked through this process, here is an example of what an end result might look like, as described by Monroe Diefendorf:

My pillars in order of importance are: spiritual, physical, relational, professional, social, and intellectual. In order to develop a closer spiritual relationship with God, I will have a daily prayer time and Bible reading. Physically, I want to become more fit, and I will devote time each day to exercise. I also want to lose weight until I reach the weight I was at the time of my wedding. Relationally, I want to pursue two new personal friendships, take one family vacation with my wife and children, and spend a minimum of one weekend alone with my wife semiannually. Professionally, I want to be the best that I can be in my occupation and commit to continuing my education by taking a minimum of one course annually. Socially, I will engage in and give to a minimum of one charitable activity. Intellectually, I will read a minimum of one book for recreation and attend a minimum of one cultural event quarterly.

STEP 5: SUMMARY

After having spent some time thinking about your personal wealth, you should answer the following questions:

Why do I exist? (This is your personal wealth purpose statement.)

_____

_____

_____

_____

What do I want to do with my life? (This is your personal wealth mission statement.) _____

_____

_____

_____

What will I achieve with my talents and my strengths? (This is your personal wealth vision statement.) _____

_____

_____

_____

At this point you should have defined and articulated the following:
  Core values
  Personal wealth pillars of importance/goals/priorities
  Personal wealth purpose statement
  Personal wealth mission statement
  Personal wealth vision statement

6 | Financial Wealth

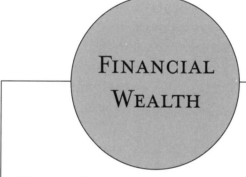

FINANCIAL WEALTH

o TAKING INVENTORY—WHAT DO YOU
CURRENTLY HAVE?

o TAKING AIM—WHAT DO YOU WANT IN THE
FUTURE?

o TAKING SHAPE—WHAT DO YOU NEED TO DO
TO GET FROM WHAT YOU
HAVE TO WHAT YOU WANT?

WHAT'S IMPORTANT ABOUT MONEY?

The second dimension, financial wealth, typically gets the most attention. Open any college catalogue and you will find an extensive curriculum that deals with money. So important is financial wealth in our culture

that financial planner was one of the top-ten careers of 2003 and 2004. Of course, of the three dimensions of wealth, financial wealth is the most tangible and most easily quantifiable. With so much written on this subject (including two books of our own that we have collaborated on), we will take a broad-brush approach to this dimension.

A key question that many one-dimensional financial planners fail to ask clients is, what's important about money? With an appreciation for the influence and power that money can have in both a positive and negative way, a clear understanding of the affects created by its use are necessary. Many planners (as well as clients) think that the more money one has the better. The standard answer to how much clients should leave their children is to minimize the amount that goes to the government and maximize the amount that goes to the family. But our experience as financial planners has shown us that you can do more harm than good by leaving *too much* financial wealth to heirs. Unless financial wealth is wrapped in the overall context of personal and social wealth, problems can develop among heirs and lasting damage to relationships can result. This damage can manifest itself in low self-esteem, low ambition, guilt, shame, disorientation, disconnectedness, and divorce. Mark 8:36 warns, "What does it profit a man if he gains the whole world but loses his soul?" How you answer the following question will determine the ultimate outcome of your personal financial purpose and mission statements.

What's so important about money? _____

_____

_____

_____

Once you have understood the importance of money in your life, you can then apply it to your financial pillars of importance.

PILLARS OF IMPORTANCE

To build a strong financial side to your structure, you must ensure that you select appropriate pillars to support your goals and priorities. Here are some possibilities:

Debt management	Risk management	Retirement
Major purchase	Estate planning	Tax planning
Accumulation	College funding	Gifting
Tithing	Cash management	Financial independence

Financial goals can be reached through proper planning and discipline with the excess cash flow and appreciation of existing assets. You do have choices, though not necessarily freedom, to use your dollars as you see fit. The flowchart below will help you understand how money works to achieve goals and how these pillars fit into your daily life.

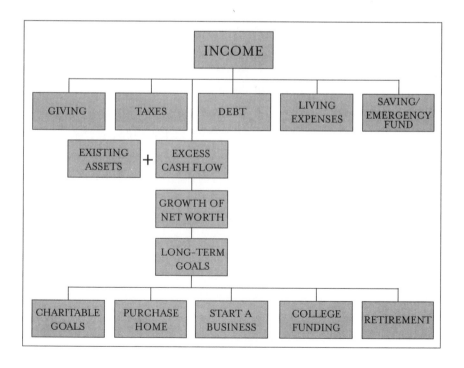

In essence, income is the engine that produces the wherewithal to give, spend, and/or save. An important concept to live by is to spend less than you make. Excess cash flow, in conjunction with previously accumulated assets, can be used to grow your financial net worth. The purpose of growing your net worth should not be for the sake of simply accumulating assets, but for a specific long-term goal that is important to you. This goal could be for the purchase of a new home, college funding for a child, or financial independence. It should be noticed that giving, saving, and spending (living expenses) are choices that you make.

Taxes are historically a civil responsibility that you have to the government in exchange for services. Although a mutual responsibility exists between taxpayer and government, there are strategies that, when utilized, allow you to give, save, and even spend more. These strategies should be considered in the planning process. Why not let Uncle Sam subsidize your investment or giving program?

One area that requires full attention is debt repayment. Debt often increases stress, which contributes to mental, physical, and emotional fatigue. It can cause harm to your personal wealth. Debt is a form of bondage unless it is "good debt."

THE RICH RULE OVER THE POOR, AND THE
BORROWER BECOMES THE LENDER'S SLAVE.
—PROVERBS 22:7

Good debt can be described in terms of borrowing money to purchase an appreciating asset, such as a business, home, or even a college education. Bad debt, as the flow chart shows, can only take away from the other alternatives, such as giving, saving, and spending, and can eliminate the potential for excess cash flow to prefund long-term goals.

Debt and lifestyle go hand in hand. When you use debt to fund a consumptive lifestyle, you do double duty damage to your financial wealth. First, the consumptive lifestyle reduces available income for important future goals and debt repayment exacerbates the problem.

There are pillars of importance inherent in the entire financial flow chart. For example, cash management is a pillar that will help you prioritize and properly budget giving, taxes, savings, debt, and living expenses. College funding and financial independence are long-term goals that are affected by excess cash flow from income and appreciation from existing assets (investment performance). It is important to understand the flows of money and how they can assist you in achieving financial wealth. But more important, you must understand what is significant about money to you and what those pillars look like.

STEP 1: IDENTIFYING THE PILLARS OF IMPORTANCE

As the architect of your financial life, list the aspects of your finances on which you wish to focus your attention. Remember, there are no wrong answers.

_____   _____   _____

_____   _____

STEP 2: TAKING INVENTORY

Taking inventory helps you to determine what you have. It is a traditional financial statement of net worth. Because financial planning is the allocation of limited financial resources to unlimited alternatives, this step will help to establish appropriate alternatives for your specific resources.

PILLARS	ASSETS	LIABILITIES
1.		
2.		
3.		
4.		
5.		

Taking inventory also answers the question, how do I use my net worth? It's a statement of your lifestyle. The number of people who actually think they "own" their financial assets is amazing. While we may have legal title to an asset, our ownership has no permanence. In reality, our financial resources are just on loan to us for a period of time that coincides with our natural lives. It is a matter of perspective and requires a fresh way of approaching our financial wealth. Stewardship is about "loanership" not "ownership." It is about accepting the responsibility to properly manage everything that God has entrusted to our care. Surely, we can pass our financial assets on to our heirs as a part of our legacy. However, it is critical that we pass on "what's important about money" as well.

STEP 3: TAKING AIM

This is about "starting with the end in mind." It is seeing in your mind's eye what your future will hold. It is about establishing specific targets (goals) that you want to hit. Creating goals creates purpose. Recording goals crystallizes your purpose. Goals are a dream with a time line, a motivation for achieving, and a statement of God's will for your life.

PILLARS	SHORT-TERM GOALS	LONG-TERM GOALS
1.		
2.		
3.		
4.		
5.		

STEP 4: TAKING SHAPE

This exercise requires you to devise strategies and prioritize each in an effort to reach your goals. Because you most likely do not have unlimited financial resources, you will be limited to the number of strategies you can employ. The hierarchy in which you order your goals is the key to your financial success. Proverbs 24:3–4 states, "By wisdom a house is built, by understanding it is established, by knowledge the rooms are filled with precious and pleasant riches." In this step you may need to seek professional assistance. A qualified financial planner will be able to provide the appropriate strategies to accomplish your personal financial goals. The planner will address all aspects of your financial life that are important to you.

Remember, this is *your* financial plan. A comprehensive financial plan will have a price tag (a planning fee), but the benefits of a well-constructed financial plan far outweigh the cost. For those "do-it-yourself" financial planners, keep in mind that to be a successful planner requires a full-time commitment to the career. Would you want to go to a part-time lawyer or doctor? However, it is important to become knowledgeable in your financial affairs so that you will be a prudent person in putting your "total wealth" plan together.

PILLARS	PRIORITY	STRATEGIES	RANK
1.			
2.			
3.			
4.			
5.			

Now that you have worked through this process, here is an example of what an end result might look like, as described by Monroe Diefendorf:

My pillars are ranked in order of their importance to me: debt management, cash management (including charitable contributions), risk management, education savings, retirement planning, and estate planning.

My goal is to live free of debt and not use my credit cards for anything more than I can cover on a monthly basis. In addition, I want to pay off all of my mortgages by the time I am sixty years old. To accomplish this objective, I will make semimonthly mortgage payments. To better manage cash, I will establish a monthly budget. In addition, I will keep an accounting of all expenses. To accomplish this, I will use an accounting program, similar to Quicken, to track all income and expenses and review my income versus expenses statement quarterly. I will establish a formalized pattern for giving money to charity. To minimize the risks in accomplishing my financial objectives, I will analyze my insurance needs (including life, health, disability, long-term care, homeowners, auto, and liability [umbrella]) and determine appropriate coverage. If I need help establishing a comprehensive plan, I will seek professional advice.

I will provide the best possible education for my three children. Initially, my goal is to fund 75 percent of the expenses of a private four-year college. To reach this goal, I will establish Sec. 529 (tax-deferred college savings) educational plans for the children contributing gifts of $11,000, the maximum tax-free gift allowed per individual per year, to each child's 529 account[1].

Retirement (or financial independence) by age sixty with an income of 80 percent of current income (adjusted at 3 percent for inflation) is another of my goals. This will initially require that my wife and I put the maximum allowed into our 401(k) plans. In addition, I will establish "moderate growth" asset allocations for these qualified plans and rebalance funds quarterly.

After providing for my wife's financial independence, 50 percent of the remaining assets will be left to my children. The 50 percent interest will be divided into two sections: a) one third to the children, "no questions asked" and b) two thirds to establish a Family Values Incentive Trust / Family Bank (see chapter 11). With the other 50 percent, a Family Foundation (see chapter 12) will be set up to provide a mechanism for family charitable giving with the children as trustees.

---

1 Qualified expenses include tuition, fees, room and board, books and other supplies needed to attend an institution of higher education. A 10 percent federally mandated penalty or additional tax applies on any earnings you withdraw for nonqualified expenses. Under a "sunset provision," the tax exemption for earnings on qualified withdrawals is scheduled to expire on December 31, 2010, unless extended by Congress. As with all tax-related decisions, consult your tax advisor.

Step 5: Summary

Financial wealth means different things to different people. The goal for you in this chapter is to come away with a fresh look at this one dimension of your life and to determine answers for the following questions:

What's important about money? (This is your financial wealth purpose statement.) _____

_____

_____

_____

What do I want to do with my financial assets? (This is your financial wealth mission statement.) _____

_____

_____

_____

What do I hope to achieve with my financial assets? (This is your financial wealth vision statement.) _____

_____

_____

_____

At this point you should have defined and articulated the following:
    Core values
    Financial wealth pillars of importance/goals/priorities
    Financial wealth purpose statement
    Financial wealth mission statement
    Financial wealth vision statement

7 | Social Wealth

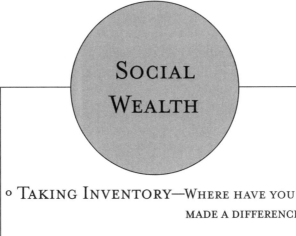

SOCIAL
WEALTH

○ TAKING INVENTORY—WHERE HAVE YOU
MADE A DIFFERENCE?

○ TAKING AIM—WHERE AND HOW DO YOU
WANT TO MAKE A DIFFERENCE?

○ TAKING SHAPE—WHAT MUST YOU DO TO
MAKE THAT DIFFERENCE?

HOW WILL YOU MAKE A DIFFERENCE?

The third dimension is by far the most exciting because it affects family, friends, and the public. Social wealth can be passed on physically, socially, morally, or spiritually, and it makes the world a better place. You are here for a purpose and social wealth correlates with that purpose. The way in which your talents are used and your money is spent relates to your appreciation for life and the legacy you desire to leave behind.

In 1943, Abraham Maslow developed the hierarchy of needs, the theory of human motivation as it relates to our human development. After the basic physiological (survival) and safety needs are satisfied, he suggested that social needs, esteem needs, and ultimately self-actualization become the driving forces in one's life. When we consider our social wealth, we must understand how and why we act and react to various human behaviors. In addition, we must understand what it is that motivates people to behave in certain ways. There are basically four human desires that strongly motivate each of us in terms of passing on our social wealth:

A DESIRE FOR INDEPENDENCE: a desire to live our lives as we see fit; to raise our families without interference; for the opportunity to rise to whatever social and economic level of which we are capable (as Americans we often take this for granted).

A DESIRE TO HELP OTHERS: a desire to do as much as we possibly can to alleviate need, deprivation, and suffering both locally and globally.

A DESIRE TO FEEL SIGNIFICANT: a desire to know that our lives have meaning; that we can contribute something to this world; that we have made an impact; that we can be influential; to know that life is not merely the result of a "lottery," with winners and losers.

A DESIRE TO FIND IMMORTALITY: a desire to know that the way my life is lived has significance beyond death; that the value of my accomplishments transcends my death.

The depth of these desires relates to success in achieving social wealth. Will the world be a better place because your time and money are invested in your passionate cause or someone else's life? Will your family enjoy a greater legacy because of the core values and vision you pass on? Suppose Noah had built his ark just big enough for his wife and children and their spouses. What would the animal kingdom be like now? Would it even exist? What challenges do you face for you to make a difference? Will you leave the world a better place than you found it? Will you discover your specific pillars of significance so that you can make a difference? Will you create and maintain a legacy that your family can pass on to future generations?

Do you want to make a difference? If the answer is yes, how will you make a difference? Whether you have fair winds and following seas in your life, or you are buffeted by contrary winds, remember, while you cannot control nature, you can control your attitudes and actions.

Once you have understood the importance of making a difference in your life, you can then apply it to your social pillars of importance.

PILLARS OF IMPORTANCE

We have listed several pillars of importance that you might consider. They address the questions of how you would like to make a difference or how would you like to be remembered.

Service to others	Voluntary philanthropy	Caregiving
Sharing and giving of time	Involuntary philanthropy	Family legacy
Servant leadership	Commitment to cause	Spiritual legacy
Teaching and mentoring	Pastoring and counseling	

STEP 1: IDENTIFY THE PILLARS OF IMPORTANCE

As you carefully ponder your social life, take time to list the areas that interest you most. If you are like most people, you will have more interests than you have time to pursue. More than simply listing, ranking the importance of your interests is critical for you to be on-purpose.

_____   _____   _____

_____   _____

STEP 2: TAKING INVENTORY

While financial wealth is a statement of your lifestyle, social wealth is a statement of your "heart style." You must ask yourself what you have done with your life to benefit others, what investment in time you have made to benefit others, and if you really care about others.

Remember, personal worth is your self-worth, financial wealth is your net worth, and social wealth is your selfless worth.

PILLARS	WHAT HAVE I DONE TO BENEFIT OTHERS
1.	
2.	
3.	
4.	
5.	

STEP 3: TAKING AIM

Taking aim requires you to look at all the pillars of importance and decide which are really important. In taking aim, you are going to set priorities for your life.

If you were to die tonight, what would you want written on your tombstone for the world to see? What would you want family members and close friends to say at your funeral? Matthew 25:23 reads: "Well done, thou good and faithful servant." Will God say the same to you?

Mortality is certain. What is not certain is the impact or legacy that your life has made on those you leave behind. To articulate your vision for social wealth, write your own obituary as you would like to be remembered.

_____

_____

_____

_____

Step 4: Taking Shape

At this time, while the strategies may not be clear to you to accomplish your objectives, it is key to list and rank these objectives.

PILLARS	STRATEGIES
1.	
2.	
3.	
4.	
5.	

Now that you have worked through this process, here is an example of what an end result might look like, as described by Monroe Diefendorf:

My pillars are ranked in order of importance: family legacy, spiritual legacy, voluntary philanthropy, mentoring, and service to others. My goal is to leave a family legacy. To do so, I will make every effort to be present at as many of my children's life events as possible. These may include sporting events, school programs, and religious ceremonies. In addition, I will commit to "creating memories" by taking a special family vacation annually. To leave a spiritual legacy, I will make weekly church attendance a priority. I will lead my family by example by studying the scriptures each morning. Also, I will make our home available to missionaries who are on furlough to expose my family to cross-cultural experiences. With a choice of voluntary versus involuntary philanthropy (social programs provided by the government), I will take steps to ensure that my charitable interests are followed. I intend to establish a private foundation that will distribute 5 percent of the income generated from my contributions. It is my desire to share my life experiences with those who come after me. To this end, I will select one business associate who I will train as my successor. As service to others, I will select Habitat for Humanity as my outlet for serving those who are less fortunate.

Step 5: Summary

Social wealth is the dimension of your wealth that provides the outlet for helping others. The goal for you in this chapter is to come away with a fresh look at this one dimension of your life and to determine answers for the following questions:

How can I make a difference with my life? (This is your social wealth purpose statement.) _____

_____

_____

_____

What do I want to do with my social assets? (This is your social wealth mission statement.) _____

_____

_____

_____

What do I hope to achieve with my social assets? (This is your social wealth vision statement.) _____

_____

_____

_____

At this point you should have defined and articulated the following:
    Core values
    Social wealth pillars of importance/goals/priorities
    Social wealth purpose statement
    Social wealth mission statement
    Social wealth vision statement

8 | BUILDING YOUR FOUNDATION

By understanding the requirements to build a permanent structure, you can put together a picture, or blueprint, of your 3 Dimensional life. When you design and construct a structure with the features listed below, many of you, for the first time, will be required to define what is really important to you. These parameters will help reduce anxiety and ease the decision-making process. Built to last, a sound structure is essential to success.

Foundations are the core values of your existence and form the base of your structure. Your purpose and mission statements, the sill and the lintel, rest on your priorities, the pillars, and define how you are to live your life. Your vision statement, the truss, rests on the purpose and mission statements and is the key to your final destination. These essential structural elements are enclosed within the walls—your attitudes and beliefs—of your structure.

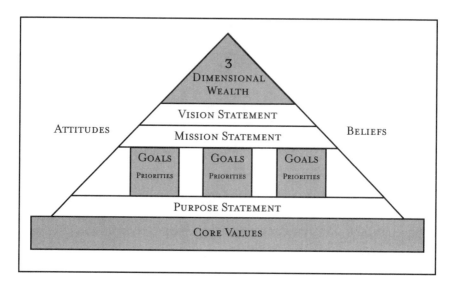

The personal, financial, and social dimensions have their own structures. Personal wealth is the "who you are" wealth; financial wealth is the "stuff you own" wealth; and social wealth measures the "making a difference" wealth. When you combine all three structures, you enter the zone called 3 Dimensional Wealth. This approach is based on a common foundation, synchronized purpose, and mission and vision statements with well-defined goals and priorities. You are the architect and builder for your 3 Dimensional structure. Our function is to facilitate its construction. The results will be significant because they will be based on your parameters.

We have discussed the three dimensions: personal, financial, and social. We advocate a common base of core values for each of the wealth dimensions. The following chart helps to organize the thinking process. Each dimension of your wealth will have separate and distinct purpose, vision, and mission statements. When you complete the assignment, you will arrive at the end of your 3 Dimensional Wealth journey with each dimension clearly defined.

	PERSONAL Wealth	FINANCIAL Wealth	SOCIAL Wealth
STEP 1: YOUR UNIFIED CORE VALUES			
STEP 2: YOUR PURPOSE STATEMENT			
STEP 3: TAKING INVENTORY			
STEP 4: TAKING AIM			
STEP 5: TAKING SHAPE			
STEP 6: YOUR VISION STATEMENT			
STEP 7: YOUR MISSION STATEMENT			

The self-discovery process reinforces your understanding of the three dimensions and their application to your life. The chart provides you with the tools you will need to create three distinct plans, one for each dimension of your life, and then integrate them into a cohesive master plan. By completing this chart you will finally have the framework for developing a total wealth plan—a 3 Dimensional Wealth plan.

As a tool to help you maintain focus on what is important, we have also provided a trifold planner, "My 3 Dimensional Wealth Plan," at the end of the book, which can easily be carried in your suit pocket or purse.

9 | SYNCHRONIZATION AND OPTIMIZATION

SYNCHRONIZING THE DIMENSIONS OF YOUR LIFE

Each activity of your daily life will fall into one of the three dimensions of your wealth. With only twenty-four hours in each day, time is a limited resource, and each dimension will be bumping into the others, vying for your attention. This friction often leads to frustration and a sense of confusion. For example, when occupied with an activity, have you ever felt like you should be doing something else? Have you ever found yourself participating in an activity that you didn't want to be involved in? It has been said that the enemy of the best is the good. How do you say no to "good" activities unless you have determined which activities are good and which activities are the best to devote your time to? Often, without well-planned goals, competing activities can lead to inertia. By not knowing what to do first, you can end up doing nothing at all.

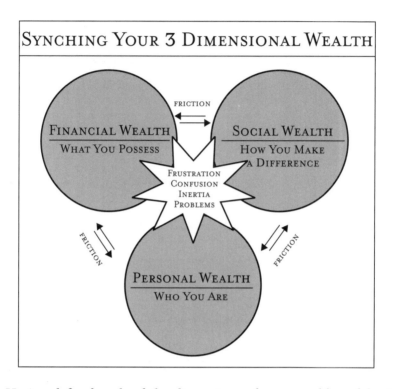

Having defined each of the dimensions of your wealth and having articulated your mission, vision, and purpose statements, you are now equipped to "synchronize" each of these dimensions. Synching the dimensions of your wealth means participating in an activity that simultaneously fulfills your goals in more than one dimension of your wealth. When you transform your life from one-dimensional fulfillment to this multilevel approach, your goal becomes achieving 100 percent unification of all three dimensions so that the circles overlap completely and all friction is eliminated. This may seem like a lofty goal. Like trying to walk to the horizon, it may seem you will never be able to reach your objective. But if you fail to incorporate this multilevel approach you can cause real problems in your life and the lives of those around you, such as anxiety and frustration, which can lead to low self-esteem.

Moreover, if you have not synchronized the dimensions of your life, as you seek to pass on the three dimensions of your wealth and create a legacy for your family, the same friction may exist. One-dimensional estate planning deals with the money you will leave behind, but how do you pass on the values and wisdom you possess? How can you define and articulate them so that they will benefit your family?

People will do everything they can to insure the financial wealth they possess. They may buy insurance to protect their homes, property, and lives. But what do they do to ensure that their social wealth is protected? What do they do to preserve and pass on the wisdom that they have learned during their lifetimes?

Personal wealth has historically been preserved by the oral and written word. Financial wealth has typically been protected by wills, trusts, and insurance. Social wealth has traditionally been protected by the use of charitable trusts or private foundations. But are there ways to synchronize these three dimensions to create a legacy that is multidimensional? The answer is yes.

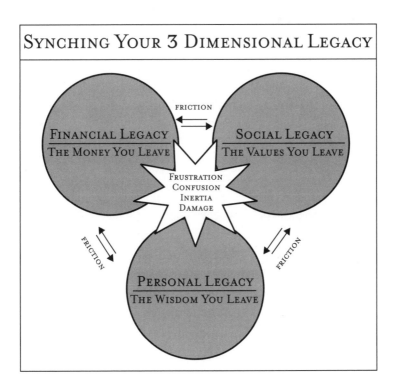

You have probably already realized that we are talking about learning a balancing act. You will learn how to juggle the 3 Dimensional Wealth balls—the unification of purpose, mission, and vision. We have developed a methodology that will help you monitor your progress.

Our goal is to challenge the status quo and ask you to reorder your world based on a 3 Dimensional mindset. Think about how much less stress you would have in your life if you were on track towards achieving your personal, financial, and social goals simultaneously. The Complementary Test is a crude way to quantify the activities of your daily living. It is a way to determine if you are living your life with a minimum amount of friction and a maximum amount of satisfaction.

THE COMPLEMENTARY TEST

Our hypothesis is that an activity is purposeful when its completion leads to the fulfillment of a stated goal. When completion of the activity leads to the satisfaction of two goals within two dimensions of your wealth, the activity has a greater degree of purposefulness. When completion of the activity leads to the satisfaction of three goals within each of the three dimensions of your wealth, the activity provides the highest satisfaction and maximum efficiency. A mathematical procedure for calculating your 3 Dimensional Wealth ratio using the Complementary Test is explained below with sample worksheets provided on the following pages.

THE COMPLEMENTARY TEST PROCEDURE

1. List each of the strategies you developed as a result of working through the taking aim exercises. Remember this includes personal, financial, and social dimensions.
2. Determine if the fulfillment (taking action) of these strategies will improve your wealth in one, two, or three (financial, personal, or social) wealth categories.
3. Place the number 1 in the appropriate column.
4. Total each row and total each column.

Strategy	Financial Wealth	Social Wealth	Personal Wealth	Totals
1 Family Foundation	1	1	1	3
2 Client Golf	1	0	1	2
3 Social Golf	0	0	1	1
4 Watch TV	0	0	0	0
5 Family Vacation	0	1	1	2
6 Church Schoolteacher	0	1	1	2
7 Job	1	0	1	2
8 Professional Designation	1	0	1	2
9 Irrevocable Life Insurance Trust	1	0	0	1
10 Mission Trip	1	1	1	3
Totals	6	4	8	18

The rows are numeric tools that allow you to see which dimensions of your wealth are being utilized effectively. A score of 1 indicates that your strategy is one dimensional. If it is an important strategy, think of ways to add additional dimensions to its utilization. As an example, if your goal is to be a world-renowned violinist, you could simply use these talents to earn a living. However, you could also use your skills to mentor a student and perform a benefit concert to raise money for orphans. The same activity, if well thought out and properly structured, could land a score of 3.

The numeric totals in the columns will help you determine which dimension occupies your time and energy. Comparing the columns might help you in determining if you are out of balance. This will give you the opportunity to rebalance as appropriate. By the way, you are the scorekeeper. This is simply a tool to help you think in three dimensions.

Another way of looking at this is through the balance ratio exercises.

THE BALANCE RATIO

1. Arithmetic weightings: This is simply the totals from each individual (e.g., financial) column divided by the total of all rows (6/18=33.33 percent).
2. Deviation from the mean: If all three dimensions had equal importance they would all have a value of 33.33 percent. To determine the deviation (either above or below), take the actual arithmetic weighting and subtract it from 33.33 percent.

3 DIMENSIONAL WEALTH BALANCE RATIO			
3 DIMENSIONAL WEALTH BALANCE RATIO	FINANCIAL	SOCIAL	PERSONAL
Arithmetic Weightings	33.33%	22.22%	44.44%
Actual Deviation from the Mean of 33.33%	0.00%	-11.11%	11.11%

This example indicates that there is an underweighting in your social wealth and an overweighting in your personal wealth.

The formulas required to complete the 3 Dimensional Wealth Balance Ratio are outlined on the following page. A blank chart is provided on page 80 so that you can complete the exercise.

Strategy	Financial Wealth	Social Wealth	Personal Wealth	Totals
1				
2				
3				
4				
5				
6				
7				
8				
9				
10				
Totals	A	B	C	D

3 Dimensional Wealth Balance Ratio			
3 Dimensional Wealth Balance Ratio	Financial	Social	Personal
Arithmetic Weightings	A/D = E	B/D = F	C/D = G
Actual Deviation from the Mean of 33.33%	E–0.333 = H	F–0.333 = J	G–0.333 = K

Strategy	Financial Wealth	Social Wealth	Personal Wealth	Totals
1				
2				
3				
4				
5				
6				
7				
8				
9				
10				
Totals				

3 Dimensional Wealth Balance Ratio			
3 Dimensional Wealth Balance Ratio	Financial	Social	Personal
Arithmetic Weightings			
Actual Deviation from the Mean of 33.33%			

Optimization and Synchronization in Action

During a recent vacation to Florida, Roey and his wife, Chris, wanted to buy a Mother's Day present for Chris's mom. Instead of going to the mall, they went to a private residence Chris had heard about where an elderly woman and her ten-year-old granddaughter make and sell handbags. In the workshop there were dozens of bags "in process." The grandma said that she supplied all of the materials but that the bags were made in a joint effort. She also told how 50 percent of the proceeds from each sale was given to charity and 50 percent was saved for a boat for the granddaughter.

It was obvious from the grandma's home that she had the resources to buy any size boat for her granddaughter, but with this simple exercise grandma was able to pass on her personal wealth during their times together in the workshop; promote and encourage her granddaughter's social wealth by showing her how to be outwardly focused through philanthropy; and teach a lesson about financial wealth through savings and thrift. What an excellent example of positive grandparenting. This simple activity of making handbags both optimized and synchronized the three dimensions of grandma's wealth and scored a perfect 3 on the Complementary Test.

SUMMARY

It is clear that you are who you are based on your core values. Your core values provide the foundation on which your life, in all three dimensions, is built and will continue to be built. We invited you to begin your journey looking through a lens that would alter the way you view your life and challenge you to step out of a one-dimensional world. This is necessary because in your natural life you are led by desire and things that make you feel good immediately. Although always being instantly gratified might sound like a wonderful world in which to live, it is most often a world of deception. This deception fosters belief that you own your material things and that the measurement of success rests purely on your tangible financial assets. Deception leads to disobedience, causing you to stray from your core values, and disobedience ultimately leads to death—both spiritual and physical.

When you view life through a 3 Dimensional Wealth lens, you begin to refocus. Rather than being led by desire, you are led by your vision, your mission, and your sense of purpose. You will not be sidetracked or deceived because the strength of your lens allows you to view life through your six paradigms. Here's a reminder:

The Six Paradigms

1. Inwardly focused is out. Outwardly focused is in.

2. Balance sheet accounting is out. Balanced life accounting is in.

3. Spend, save, then give is out. Give, save, then spend is in.

4. Immediate gratification is out. Future gratification is in.

5. Ownership is out. Stewardship is in.

6. One-dimensional wealth is out. 3 Dimensional Wealth is in.

Having gone through the process of exploring the three dimensions of your wealth, these paradigms should now make more sense. By adhering to these paradigms your course will take you to a life of obedience, not disobedience. It would be extremely difficult to lead a life of obedience if the source of your life, the essence of your being, comes from yourself. An "anything goes" approach to life means being obedient to your own desires and wishes, which is about as one-dimensional as you can get.

The Legacy You Leave

Introduction

Taking what you have learned and putting it into practice is not as easy to do as you might like. If it were, we could all be golf pros after a few lessons. If you are serious about wanting to change your life, it is important to immediately act on what you have learned. The process has been clearly outlined for you. It is up to you to put it in motion.

Refer to the self-discovery process, when you took inventory of each dimension of your wealth, and the Complementary Test that helped you determine if you are optimizing your actions. Now, you must understand what 3 Dimensional Wealth is telling you.

You will discover, as we have, that there is a seemingly unnatural order of events that must be followed to achieve 3 Dimensional success. Television ads tell us that a spending lifestyle is the secret to happiness. Our financial advisors tell us that we should save approximately 10–15 percent of our income in order to achieve financial independence later in life. What remains is discretionary income that can be used to spend, save, or be given away.

Time out!

This order is an example of traditional, one-dimensional thinking, and one-dimensional thinking is backwards. The 3 Dimensional Wealth meth-hod is a radically sane way to approach your wealth. Remember the 3 Dimensional Wealth paradigm that states: give first, save second, and spend third. If there is money left over, you can give more and save more, or spend it if it adds to your financial, personal, or social success. But what makes this approach sane? The authors believe that this unconventional order is based on biblical principles and that's what makes it sane, practical, and applicable to us today.

ONE MAN GIVES FREELY, YET GAINS EVEN MORE;
ANOTHER WITHHOLDS UNDULY, BUT COMES
TO POVERTY. A GENEROUS MAN WILL PROSPER;
HE WHO REFRESHES OTHERS WILL HIMSELF
BE REFRESHED.

—PROVERBS 11:24–25

Another way of thinking about 3 Dimensional Wealth "giving" is investing. You may ask how giving something away can be considered investing. When you give to a cause, a person, or an institution, you are making an investment because that contribution will grow in social value. The gift is similar to teaching someone how to fish rather than simply giving the person a fish. Giving is a wonderful act and can be equated to investing. The problem is no school exists to teach you why or how to give. Therefore, we've provided a primer.

You are familiar with giving from a financial wealth perspective, but let's discuss giving as an integral part of your personal and social wealth. When you gift your talents and time to make this world a better place to live, you strengthen your life structure. If you think in 3 Dimensional terms, giving financially + giving personally + giving socially = 3 Dimensional success.

You may wonder how you can use the same dollar to satisfy and achieve your gifting objectives in more than one dimension of your wealth simultaneously. The answer lies in relying on basic core values that are the foundation to all decisions you make. This means that you do not give to any causes that do not align with those values. Your attitudes and beliefs are also factors that must be aligned. It is of significant importance to ensure that your social wealth pillars are in place so that you can prioritize your giving. Your giving must also align with your purpose, mission, and vision statements. Finally, what complementary score is achieved in this giving program? Is it acceptable? You must get serious about your giving, just as you are about your spending and saving. Calculating a gift impact factor will help you determine if your giving aligns with your values.

The gift impact factor is a tool to measure the optimization of your 3 Dimensional gifting. It works like this:

1. List all of your gifting projects.
2. List the dollar amounts you desire to gift.
3. Give a "priority factor" number. This is accomplished by ranking the projects by their level of importance:

> 1 = You do not consider your gift an investment, but a socially necessary act.
>
> 2 = You consider your gift an investment aligned with your values and convictions.
>
> 3 = You consider your gift an investment that perpetuates your legacy and maintains your values.

4. Determine the gift impact factor by multiplying the gift amount by the priority factor.
5. The highest score on the gift impact factor will determine the level of priority.

A sample gift impact factor worksheet provided on the next page illustrates the concept.

GIFT OPPORTUNITY	(A) GIFT AMOUNT	(B) PRIORITY FACTOR	(AxB) GIFT IMPACT FACTOR	PRIORITY RANKING
1 Library Drive	$250	1	$250	5
2 Fire Department Drive	$25	1	$25	7
3 Zambia Orphanage	$1,500	2	$3,000	2
4 Church Building Project	$750	3	$2,250	3
5 The Family Foundation	$2,000	3	$6,000	1
6 Alma Mater Annual Gift	$100	2	$200	6
7 Hospital Research Project	$1,000	2	$2,000	4
8				
9				
10				

Factor your own gift impact factor with the worksheet provided below. This exercise will help reveal your most important gifting opportunities. Have some fun discovering the joy of giving.

GIFT OPPORTUNITY	(A) GIFT AMOUNT	(B) PRIORITY FACTOR	(AxB) GIFT IMPACT FACTOR	PRIORITY RANKING
1				
2				
3				
4				
5				
6				
7				
8				
9				
10				

> ## THE NECESSITY OF A STRATEGY
>
> WITH RESPECT TO THE TOTALITY OF YOUR FAMILY WEALTH,
>
> HOW WILL YOU SPECIFICALLY
>
> CAPTURE IT, ENHANCE IT, PRESERVE IT, AND PERPETUATE IT?

Remember: personal wealth + financial wealth + social wealth = 3 Dimensional Wealth.

In summary, giving is a way of continuing, or perpetuating your wealth. Since each dimension of your wealth has value, you must explore methods of perpetuating your total wealth.

The following three chapters introduce methods of perpetuation. Resources for obtaining additional information are listed in the appendix.

10 | GIFTING YOUR PERSONAL WEALTH

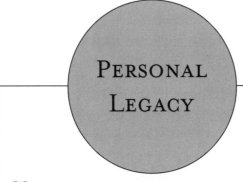

PERSONAL LEGACY

○ WHAT VALUE COULD THE WISDOM YOU HAVE ACCUMULATED OVER A LIFETIME OF EXPERIENCES HAVE TO YOUR CHILDREN AND GRANDCHILDREN?

○ WHAT STRATEGY WILL YOU EMPLOY TO PROTECT THIS ASSET?

What value could the wisdom you have accumulated over a lifetime be to your children and grandchildren? It is the intangible assets of the mind along with the life lessons you pass on that can make a significant difference to future generations. It has been said that the smart man learns from his own mistakes, but the wise man learns from the mistakes of others. Since your wisdom has priceless value, you must discover what strategies you will employ to protect this asset.

We are so concerned about our financial assets that we create wills and trusts to protect and distribute them. We buy insurance on our homes, cars, and our lives to protect these tangible assets. But rarely, if ever, do we see a strategic plan for an individual to protect and perpetuate his or her personal wealth. If your life is worth living, it's worth recording, and the tools exist to create such a legacy.

Techniques Used to Capture, Enhance, Preserve, and Perpetuate Personal Legacy	
Oral Tradition	Audio Recorded
Written Word	Video Recorded

Historically, individuals and families have relied on storytelling to pass on personal wealth from generation to generation. But memories quickly fade and one's wisdom, values, beliefs, and lessons become distorted over time or forgotten.

Many write autobiographies or memoirs to pass on their heritages. Some create family albums. Do either of these really get to the core of your personal wealth? Do these formats really preserve and protect your personal legacy? We have created a document that attempts to capture this dimension of your wealth.

The Family Legacy Manuscript Is Born

As part of our entry into the world of 3 Dimensional Wealth, Monroe Diefendorf, Jr., created The Foundation for the Preservation & Encouragement of Family Values, LLC. This organization's mission is to help individuals pass on their personal wealth through the creation of a comprehensive document that encompasses the length, width, and depth of one's life. Individuals cover the following areas when creating their comprehensive documents or manuscripts:

Heritage: Describe your ancestors as far back as you can recall and include historical documents that enhance your recollection. Suggestions include: where they originated, their varied occupations, any unique characteristics or special accomplishments that have shaped your family through the generations.

Personal life: This includes specific stories and anecdotes that will encapsulate the essence of who you are.

Married life: This journey begins with your meeting, your courting days, your wedding, your early years of marriage, your child-rearing days, and your harvest years with your spouse, emphasizing important milestones and/or turning points.

Financial: This includes the formula you have used to create your financial wealth. In addition, we hope to capture your definition of the meaning of wealth and how you intend to use it (for yourself, your family, and for others).

Spiritual life: Here is your opportunity to articulate precisely what your inner self is saying. This is the most personal part of the manuscript and is an excellent venue for you to express what is in your heart for future generations.

Social life: This section will allow you to describe how service to others has affected your family. Specific examples are encouraged and philanthropic legacies should be discussed.

Closing comments: This is your chance to summarize what you believe your family is about and what you hope it continues to become throughout the twenty-first century and beyond.

With each area that you cover, be sure to highlight life lessons that you wish to leave as your personal legacy.

You may be asking yourself if you are able to create this kind of manuscript on your own. Of course you can, but will you? You haven't done it to date! The fact that seven out of eight people die intestate (without preparing a last will and testament) is a good indicator that few, if any, will actually articulate the most important elements of their lives to their families. Don't think it, ink it!

Also consider more technical ways of preserving a legacy. Audio recordings, and video and film recordings are also effective ways to capture the personality of a family member.

One last comment: we believe there is a proper delivery of one's family legacy manuscript. A family retreat is the ideal setting for sharing your personal wealth and your personal legacy. By learning how to gift your personal wealth, you will have established the first dimension of your 3 Dimensional legacy.

11 | GIFTING YOUR FINANCIAL WEALTH

FINANCIAL LEGACY

○ HOW MUCH MONEY SHOULD YOU LEAVE YOUR CHILDREN AND GRANDCHILDREN?

○ WHY AND HOW SHOULD YOU LEAVE THAT AMOUNT TO THEM?

○ WHAT IMPACT DO YOU THINK IT MIGHT HAVE ON THEM?

One-dimensional financial planners are trained to suggest that a client minimize the amount left to the government and maximize the amount left to the family. While this type of estate planning might be efficient in putting more money in the hands of the successive generations, it fails to address the psychological and emotional power that money has on individuals and families. Studies have shown that too much money, especially in the hands of very young adults (children) can do more harm than good. Often there is a lack of self-esteem that goes along with inherited money. It can also manifest itself in feelings of shame and guilt. It even rears its ugly head through the lack of humility that accompanies an opulent lifestyle. The parent or grandparent might have thought that a large bundle of cash might help their successors get a leg up in life, but it may have just the opposite effect. Lack of initiative and drive can be a result of too much of a good thing. Warren Buffett puts it this way: "I want to leave my children enough so that they can do anything they want but not enough so that they don't have to do anything at all."

The *why* and *how* questions regarding money you left to children and grandchildren open up a wide array of feelings. If money alone is left to children, without being left in a wrapper of personal wealth (wisdom) and social wealth (values), more often than not your children will end up with financial problems. The wealth syndrome suggests that one will never have enough money, earned or inherited. It becomes a matter of putting your wealth in the proper context. It's been said that there are two ways you can be rich: one is to have all you want and the other is to be satisfied with what you have. We recommend you determine how much is enough for your children and grandchildren and work your financial and estate plans from that starting point. Once you have arrived at an appropriate amount to leave to your children or grandchildren, how do you do it? Do you leave a lump sum? Do you allow them to make decisions at the age of majority (age eighteen or twenty-one)? Is there a way to protect your heirs from themselves?

There are many techniques available to distribute wealth to younger generations, but they are beyond the scope of this book. The appendix lists several resource books that will help you in this area. However, there is one "advanced" technique that merits a brief discussion—The Family Values Legacy Trust/Family Bank.

TOOLS AND TECHNIQUES USED TO CAPTURE, ENHANCE, PRESERVE, AND PERPETUATE FINANCIAL LEGACY

WILLS	FAMILY DYNASTY TRUSTS
LIVING TRUSTS	OFFSHORE TRUSTS
CREDIT SHELTER TRUSTS	FAMILY VALUES LEGACY TRUST/FAMILY BANK
ILITs	
FLPs, QPRTs, GRITs, GRATs	

THE FAMILY VALUES LEGACY TRUST/FAMILY BANK

This advanced technique is split into two parts: Tier I and Tier II. This type of trust provides for financial stability yet allows for independent decision-making as one's 3 Dimensional Wealth matures.

FAMILY LEGACY VALUES TRUSTS

TIER 1: NO QUESTIONS ASKED
- ANNUAL INCOME (MODEST)
- AGE-BASED PRINCIPAL DISTRIBUTIONS

TIER 2: VALUES-BASED INCENTIVES
- TUITION MATCHING PROGRAM
- EARNINGS MATCH
- OCCUPATIONAL INCOME ASSISTANCE
- BUSINESS VENTURE CAPITAL PROGRAM
- FAMILY VACATION FUND

Tier I: No Questions Asked

Once you determine how much you want to leave, you are ready to address how you want to leave it. This approach allows some portion of your assets to be left with no strings attached. For example, your child will receive one third of your assets—no questions asked. Our experience has led us to the conclusion that these sums should be left in stages rather than in a lump sum. The fund will provide income to the child until age forty. At age twenty-five, one fourth of the account will be distributed to the child. At age thirty, one third of the remaining fund will be distributed. At age thirty-five, one half of the remaining fund will be distributed. Finally, at age forty, the total account balance will be distributed to the child. This protects against false starts at early ages. It allows the child to grow into responsibility as it relates to financial wealth.

Tier II: Values-Based Incentives Trust/Family Bank

First and foremost, this is not an attempt to rule from the grave. It is a tool designed to expand, not restrict heirs' activities. The following example clarifies this point.

An elementary school's playground was adjacent to a highway. When the children went out at recess to play, they would use only two thirds of the field, leaving a large buffer zone to the highway. The school board subsequently put a fence around the playground, which appeared to limit the play area. However, the children played right up to the fence, thus actually expanding their territory!

And so it is with the Values-Based Incentive Trust/Family Bank. It sets boundaries that liberate, not restrict. It helps frame your financial wealth in the context of your personal and social wealth wrappers. Many children and grandchildren who have substantial inherited wealth take a well-intentioned asset and turn it into a liability. What if you could eliminate the friction that money and finances may create in a marriage or a relationship?

For example, a young lady is left a trust fund with unrestricted use. What happens when her new husband's best friend's second cousin comes up with a "business" venture that needs capital investors? Does this create an unnecessary strain on the relationship if the new bride feels the money is "daddy's" money and it should not be touched? What if the Values-Based Incentive Trust/Family Bank had a business venture capital program that encouraged entrepreneurship and small business ventures. Then, maybe 50 percent of the trust could be used to fund a new business venture provided there was a written business plan that would be approved by the Small Business Administration or the local bank for financing. Then, when the request is made to invest in "the hot new deal," the young wife can say, "Sure, but we just need to make sure that it fits the provisions of a prudent business venture." These parameters are designed to allow heirs to "play right up to the fence."

How about an occupational income assistance program in your family bank? The provisions may provide an income subsidy if certain lower-income occupations were chosen as a profession such as a missionary, a social worker, or perhaps even full-time mother. This program allows children to select careers that interest them instead of a higher-paying career forced upon them for financial reasons. Is this restrictive or liberating?

Another example is the family vacation fund. What if one of the core values of your family is to spend quality time on a regular basis? As the years go by and the children grow up and get married, their financial circumstances will differ. One may marry a rich doctor and one a witch doctor. One may have the wherewithal to travel to a location for a family gathering, while another just can't make ends meet. But what if your Values Based Incentive Trust/Family Bank provided funds available to all of your children's families, regardless of their finances, to attend a family retreat? Is this helpful or can it be harmful if it is perceived to command attendance. It does not mandate specific activities but provides funds in trust for those who wish to participate in such activities. Would having a family vacation fund accomplish gifting your financial wealth in a way that also is an investment in one's personal wealth? The answer is yes. This is the synching of your personal legacy with your financial legacy.

FAMILY LEGACY VALUES TRUST
STANDARD OR DYNASTY IRREVOCABLE TRUST

TIER 1: "NO QUESTIONS ASKED" (ONE-THIRD ALLOCATION)	TIER 2: "VALUES-BASED CLAUSES" (TWO-THIRDS ALLOCATION)
MODEST ANNUAL INCOME	TUITION MATCHING FUND
PRINCIPAL DISTRIBUTION—AGE 25	CHARITABLE GIVING MATCHING FUND
PRINCIPAL DISTRIBUTION—AGE 30	OCCUPATIONAL INCOME ASSISTANCE FUND
PRINCIPAL DISTRIBUTION—AGE 35	BUSINESS VENTURE CAPITAL FUND
PRINCIPAL DISTRIBUTION—AGE 40	FAMILY UNITY AND VACATION FUND
	_____ FUND

— — — — — — — — — AT TERMINATION OF TRUST (AGE 65–75)— — — — — — — — — — —

FAMILY FOUNDATION OR FAVORITE CHARITY

Do you get the idea? Less friction, more efficient. That's how 3 Dimensional Wealth works!

12 | GIFTING YOUR SOCIAL WEALTH

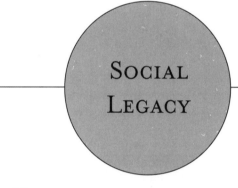

SOCIAL LEGACY

○ WHAT ROLE DID YOU PLAY IN POSITIVELY
SHAPING THIS WORLD FOR GENERATIONS
TO COME?

○ WHAT STRATEGIES HAVE YOU USED TO ASSURE
ITS CONTINUANCE?

Your values, beliefs, and convictions are three of the most powerful assets that you own. No one can take them away from you. A poor stock market or a real-estate bubble bursting will not affect this part of your balance sheet according to a 3 Dimensional Wealth view. Your core values form the base of your 3 Dimensional structure. They are the starting point of your journey. They are also at the end of the journey, so we can start at the end or the beginning. Following the roadmap to 3 Dimensional Wealth will eventually lead you to your final destination. As part of social legacy planning, individuals focus on the legacy they leave to their families and society.

I BELIEVE THAT A PERSON OUGHT TO KNOW
WHAT HE BELIEVES, WHY HE BELIEVES IT,
AND THEN BELIEVE IT.
—CHARLES "TREMENDOUS" JONES

Family members play an important role in maintaining a lasting impact on society, and including them is the goal of social legacy. Many affluent Americans are encouraging their heirs to become personally involved in charitable work and philanthropic ventures. There is growing evidence, especially among the financially wealthy, that charitable giving during the donor's lifetime is just the beginning of a social legacy that is meant to continue past the donor's death. These changing dynamics have fueled the growth of private foundations, charitable remainder trusts, charitable lead trusts, donated life insurance plans, etc. At the end of the journey, a legacy can have a lasting impact on both your heirs and society.

A GOOD NAME IS MORE DESIRABLE
THAN GREAT RICHES; TO BE ESTEEMED IS BETTER
THAN SILVER OR GOLD.
—PROVERBS 23:2

Gifting your social wealth and creating a social legacy requires values, beliefs, and convictions. Neither power, nor fame, nor money is enough. One day, Alfred Nobel, the inventor of dynamite, opened his newspaper to read of his brother's death. However, a mistake had been made and the obituary was written about Alfred himself. He was shocked that he was remembered solely as "the man who invented dynamite." He realized that his legacy was of little social significance. He subsequently established new pillars of importance and redirected his efforts to more "Nobel" things. He was determined that he would shape the world for generations to come by creating the Nobel Peace Prize.

During the social wealth discovery process we defined pillars of importance as related to selfless worth. As an example, one of these pillars might have been labeled "service to others" or "voluntary philanthropy." We took inventory of our values and beliefs. We took aim by determining what was really important to us. We then created strategies, like to serve as a caregiver or make a commitment to fight cancer; established priorities; and allowed our social wealth to take shape. Surely, if something is worth creating, it is definitely worth preserving.

Strangely, the best way to preserve what is most important to you is to give it away. By definition, you must give away social wealth. Begin this process by asking yourself what role you have played in positively shaping this world for generations to come. If you believe that the future is in the hands of youth, then you should search for ways to shape future generations through gifting. Without the principle of gifting as part of your life, you will never experience life to the fullest. True love is synchronized with giving.

YOU CAN GIVE WITHOUT LOVING, BUT YOU CAN'T LOVE WITHOUT GIVING.

Our experience as financial advisors tells us that unless a person develops a heart for giving early in life, this aspect of his life never seems to flourish. We have heard people say, "When I have it, then I will give it away." But they rarely do. They never have enough of "it." This type of person seems to have deep pockets and short arms.

What can you do to help the needy and at the same time help to develop a new generation of philanthropists? Remember, it is not the size of the gift, but the size of the heart that counts when giving away social wealth. We can all participate in this kind of legacy planning.

The second question you should ask is what lasting impact you will have on your family and on society. It is not what you say during your lifetime that speaks loudest to those around you. Politicians promise much during campaigns, but it is their actions that impact society. Your gift of social wealth makes a difference to some degree. Social legacy is all about handing down to the next generation those values that make a difference.

You should also ask what strategies you have employed to assure the continuance of your social wealth. Without a strategy to capture, enhance, preserve, protect, and transmit your social wealth, it will die with you. There will be no assurance that the commitment to your cause or the values that you cherish will flourish in the next generation unless you purposefully pass it on.

Is there a way to develop a strategy for the gifting of your social wealth? Is there a way to map your gifting program to your newly created social wealth mission statement? Yes, but you must take a proactive role.

Social capital can be broken down into two major categories: voluntary and involuntary.

Taxes are an involuntary contribution to social programs. The U.S. government is the major funding source of social programs. A percentage of each tax dollar goes to various programs: defense, 47 percent; health, education, and welfare, 34 percent; general government, 13 percent; and physical resources, 6 percent.

To take advantage of the government's OPT-OUT PROVISION on these taxes, you must take some action!

Our current tax law provides many planning tools and encourages the use of them through tax incentives. We have listed just a few below.

Tools and Techniques Used to Capture, Enhance, Preserve, and Perpetuate Social Legacy	
Outright Bequests	Charitable Lead Trusts
Charitable Remainder Trusts	Family Foundations

Full-blown versions of how each technique works is beyond the scope of this book, but equipped with your social wealth mission statement you should be motivated to learn how these tools and techniques can work for you.

The Internet and the advent of advanced technologies will facilitate the establishment of your family foundation. Five or so years ago, if a client wanted to consider establishing a private foundation, we would have suggested an initial minimum contribution of $5,000,000. Today, these foundations can be established for only $100,000! (Donor-advised funds can be established for as little as $10,000.) Family foundations can now become an important part of the financial and estate plans for a much larger group of people. Here's how it works:

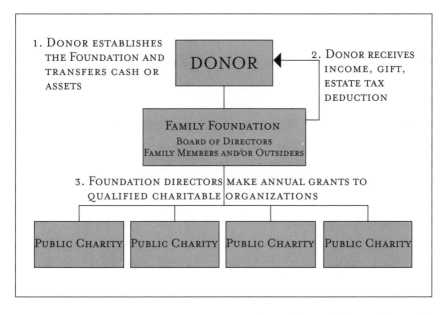

A tax-exempt corporation, or trust, is created, e.g., The ABC Family Foundation. The donor transfers assets into the foundation and receives an income, gift and/or an estate tax deduction. The foundation elects a board of directors, perhaps your spouse and your children and/or grandchildren. Your foundation is required to give away annual grants to qualified charities, i.e., 501(c) (3) organizations.

What kinds of assets can be gifted to your family foundation?

During Life:

○ Assets that are not needed to maintain your current standard of living.
○ Charitable contributions that are part of your new give, save, and spend paradigm.

At Death:

○ Your qualified retirement plan assets [IRA, 401(k), 403(b)] at the death of the surviving spouse.
○ The ultimate beneficiary of your charitable remainder trust or lead trust.
○ Your assets that would have otherwise been taxed at your death.

The IRS places some hurdles to be cleared such as a 2 percent excise tax to be paid each year to name just one. However, the price tag seems relatively small compared to the many advantages.

Private Family Foundations Advantages

Total Family Control

○ Reasonable Compensation of Family Officers
○ Reimbursement of travel expenses for conferences and "site visits"
○ Family Foundation Board Retreats
○ Greater Family Unity Building
○ Greater Family Identity

Do you know that officers of your family foundation are entitled to reasonable compensation? Are you aware that annual board meetings are required but that travel expenses (only coach fares) can be paid by your foundation? Note: There are guidelines and reasonableness is recommended when paying expenses from your foundation.

The desire to take a family retreat to help foster family unity in the years to come can accomplish multiple objectives by synching it with your personal, financial, and social wealth.

Private Family Foundations
Inter Vivos Use: Fulfillment During Life

- Income Tax Deduction
- Capital Gain Avoidance on Public Stock
- Occupational and Retirement Income Tool for Founder: Must be "Reasonable and Necessary"
- Family Unity and Identity Tool (Family Retreats)

There are many benefits to be derived from such an instrument. What better way to encourage and mentor stewardship and philanthropy than through your own family foundation? We recommend involving children and grandchildren at an early age, say fourteen and older. Allow them to attend and participate in your board meetings. Give them charitable granting authority of small amounts initially, perhaps as little as $100. It's not the amount of their gift that is important but the shaping of their characters. Remember, one day Junior is going to be sitting at the head of the table and passing on his values to his successor generations. Why not use the same skill sets to create a family philanthropic mission statement? It's a great way to teach our children to love people and use things, not vice-versa.

What a wonderful tool to be used as part of your overall financial and estate plans. The legacy that we create can have maximum impact when all three dimensions of your wealth are incorporated into a comprehensive plan.

Private Family Foundations
Testamentary Use: Legacy at Death

- Recipient of All IRD Assets at Second Death
- Recipient of All Estate Taxable Assets at Second Death
- Occupational and Lifetime Income Tool for Heirs
- Family Unity and Identity Tool (Family Retreats)
- Social Legacy and Values Perpetuation Tool

Financial advisors frequently witness the effects the death of a loved one has on families. We see the range of emotions from grief and fear, to greed and, sometimes, a peace that passes all understanding. But too often we find children and siblings fighting over who gets what. How much more meaningful a legacy would you leave if your children had to fight over what they had to *give away* rather than what they could keep?

We have created family foundation programs that involve our families in directing our social wealth. The Madden Family Foundation provides a forum for the family to meet periodically to discuss giving to "matters of significance." Bob and Cindy are the co-trustees and they have named their children as successor trustees. Both families utilize the family foundation as a tool to get their children involved now, so that they will be prepared to become the trustees of the future.

Jeremiah 8:20 contains some of the saddest words in the scriptures: ". . . the harvest is past, the summer is ended, and we are not saved." Don't let that be your legacy. Time passes swiftly. Days become months, and months become years. Get it done, now.

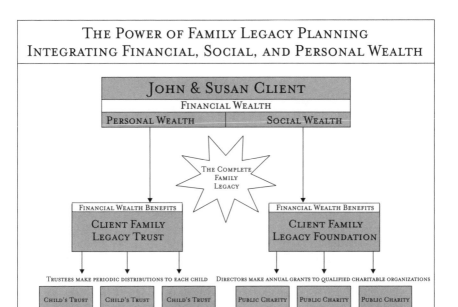

IV | CONCLUSION

13 | THE GODLY DIMENSION

The most important element of our 3 Dimensional model is what we shall call the Godly dimension. Similar to the pyramids of Egypt, it is the capstone of your life structure. It integrates the personal, financial, and social dimensions much like your core values form the foundational element of our model. The Godly dimension starts you on your voyage, propels you through life, and gives you the wherewithal to carry on day by day. Knowing God exists and having Him always present with you is critical to achieving 3 Dimensional Wealth. He is the source of your strength.

Keep the following three attributes of God in perspective: First, God is eternal. He has no beginning or end. He always has been and always will be. Second, God represents truth in its purest form, and truth sets your spirit free. When your spirit is free, you can "fly with the eagles," so to speak. Third, God generates the "juice" or power to motivate you to action and sustain you. If you want power, you must connect to the power source, much like the terminals on a battery, or the wiring of an electrical circuit. You work best when you're "plugged in" to God. You'll be energized to seek 3 Dimensional Wealth only when the connection to God is made and maintained. Eternal, true, the ultimate in power—that is our God!

IN HIS HEART A MAN PLANS HIS COURSE,
BUT THE LORD DETERMINES HIS STEPS.
—PROVERBS 16:19

Finding God is the ultimate quest in life. Where did I come from? What is the meaning of life? Why do I exist? What happens to me when I die? These are considered first order questions of life. Only God can provide the ultimate answers to these questions. You can be personally, financially, and even socially successful, but if the answers to these questions are inadequate, you experience a vague dissatisfaction, and this nagging sense of inadequacy will inhibit your achievement of 3 Dimensional Wealth.

In *A Confession*, Leo Tolstoy searched for meaning and purpose in life. The author led a promiscuous, drunken, wild life. He made lots of money and became important and famous through his books, especially *War and Peace*. However, he did not find answers to the basic questions of life or achieve fulfillment until he found God.

Why do so many people, especially our youth, feel helpless and hopeless, and approach each day with fear and anxiety. Teenage suicide rates of today are greater than last generation's. Unfortunately, those who go to this extreme truly feel that their lives don't matter. But their lives *do* matter. We were all created for a purpose.

Your mission is to find your purpose in life and then live that life to the fullest. We hope that by now you have gotten some practical methods to do just that.

Your life matters not only for today but for tomorrow as well. In fact, it matters even after you die. You will create a legacy (either by design or by default) that will last for generations to come. And you will realize your legacy to the fullest if you synchronize its three dimensions.

Mark 8:36 asks, "What does it profit a man if he gains the whole world but loses his soul?" This Bible passage clearly indicates that there is more than one dimension to life. One truly has no life without a Godly dimension. We believe that we are created with some music in our lives. We do nothing to merit it; it comes with the package. However, it is our responsibility to play that music during our lifetimes. The challenge is to take the insights that you have learned, use the strategies that have been put forth, and use these "instruments" to "play the music." Jonathan Swift puts it this way, "May you live all the days of your life."

The Godly dimension is too important to overlook. You can have wonderful core values, attitudes, and beliefs, but if you do not have a relationship with God, who is greater than all that is within you, you will have a chasm too great to fill. You will be frustrated, confused, and sapped of energy. Your paradigm lens will not be properly focused without a Godly perspective.

We encourage you to find God. He is closer than you think. He also wants to be your daily encourager, enabler, and energizer. He will put your house in order. It will be the most important decision you make on this journey, and He will help you to answer life's most difficult questions.

14 | TAKING ACTION

You have been challenged to look at life 3 Dimensionally. You have been asked to take action in several different areas of your life. If you have been diligent and disciplined you should now have the following 3 Dimensional tools in place:

3 DIMENSIONAL WEALTH PLANNING TOOLS

o Core Values, Attitudes, and Beliefs
o Pillars of Importance
o Purpose Statement
o Vision Statement
o Mission Statement
o The Complementary Test
o Gift Impact Factor

In addition, you have been challenged to "put these creeds into deeds." Live each day as if it were your last because someday you'll be right. Don't let "one of these days" become "none of these days."

> A good plan vigorously executed right now is
> far better than a perfect plan
> executed next week.
> —General George Patton

These tools are designed to add fulfillment during your life, but remember that all of the actions you take today will create a lasting legacy for tomorrow. Therefore, your 3 Dimensional Legacy planning is critical to making your life count. Our experience has shown us that very little time is spent on planning the transition of the family as compared to the transition of the family assets! While we have briefly discussed the following legacy planning tools in this book, we encourage you find a 3 Dimensional Wealth Practitioner who can help you fully discover the ways that these tools can be utilized. These tools include:

3 Dimensional Wealth Legacy Planning Tools

- The Family Legacy Manuscript
- The Family Retreat
- The Family Values Trust/Family Bank
- The Family Foundation
- The Family Mission & Philanthropic Mission Statements
- The 3 Dimensional Wealth Plan (Personal, Financial, Social)

The 3 Dimensional Wealth plan is a well–thought out process that includes all of the elements necessary in preserving your family wealth through the transition process. It is the vehicle that coordinates the legacy planning tools mentioned above into one comprehensive package. What better way to stimulate multigenerational involvement within the family and experience ultimate success in your total wealth transition?

The journey we are on has an interesting way of meeting new forks in the road, and encountering detours and tempting parking places along the way. You must not think that you have arrived at the end of your journey. This is just one leg of the trip. Recalibration is required periodically in all three dimensions. It is a lifelong journey that begins one day and continues the next, and the next, and the next.

A YEAR FROM NOW YOU MAY WISH YOU HAD STARTED TODAY.

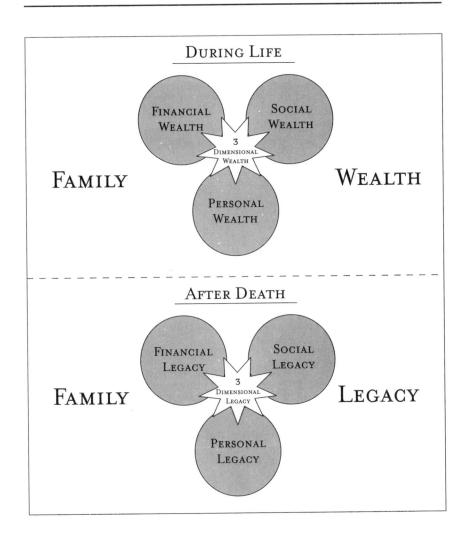

So where do we end? At the start, of course!

Stop procrastinating. Don't let one of those days become none of those days.

Take aim. If you don't have a target then your aim doesn't matter.

Act like your life depends on it. It does.

Refocus and rebalance your life. It's not too late, whatever your age.

Trust in yourself. You were made for a life of significance.

Success means living life smarter. Significance means living life fuller. And 3 Dimensional Wealth is the means to a life of significance. Remember, change is inevitable, growth is optional. So it is up to you to make your life count for today, tomorrow, and for eternity.

It is our hope that your journey through this book is the beginning of a more meaningful life.

3 Dimensionally yours,

Roey Diefendorf and Bob Madden

Appendix

Where do you go for help

This might not be as easy as you think. There are many degrees and designations that indicate a proficiency in financial wealth. However, the advisor may be one-dimensional in his or her approach to your situation. Without a working knowledge of the financial tools available, your plan will be weak at best. Therefore, it is advisable to begin your search with an advisor who has one or more of the following profesional designations:

Certified 3 Dimensional Wealth Practitioner (C3DWP): Granted by 3 Dimensional Wealth International

This advanced designation is for those who have already attained one or more of their financial designations and seek to expand their practices to include "total wealth" management capabilities, which include personal and social wealth. Course topics include: Marriage, Divorce & Family Dynamics; Stress & Career Building; Parenting & The Empty Nest; Aging, Caregiving & The Sandwich Generation; Pre- & Postretirement Counseling; Death, Dying & Bereavement; The Family Legacy Manuscript; The Family & Philanthropic Mission Statements; The Family Foundation; The Family Retreat; The 3 Dimensional Wealth Plan; Behavioral Finance Survey; and Interpersonal Relationships & Social Styles Awareness.
www.3DWealth.org

Chartered Financial Consultant (ChFC): Granted by The American College

Courses include life insurance, income taxation, planning for retirement needs, financial planning, fundamentals of estate planning, financial systems in the economy, financial-planning applications, estate-planning applications, and financial decision making at retirement.

Chartered Life Underwriter (CLU): Granted by The American College

Courses include insurance and financial planning, individual life insurance, life insurance law, fundamental of estate planning, planning for business owners and professionals, health insurance, income taxation, group benefits, retirement needs, and investment.

Certified Financial Planner (CFP): Granted by the CFP Board of Standards of the College of Financial Planning

Areas of review include financial planning, insurance and risk management, employee benefits, investment planning, income tax planning, retirement planning, and estate planning.

Certified Investment Management Analyst (CIMA): Granted by The Investment Management Consultants Association (IMCA)

Three years of experience and completion of a residence program at the Wharton School of Business, University of Pennsylvania. Course topics include: income investment policy, asset allocation, risk management, historical returns, duration and convexity, international financial markets, performance measurement and attribution, due diligence and manager selection, and legal and regulatory environment.

Chartered Financial Analyst (CFA): Granted by the Association for Investment Management and Research (AIMR)

This prestigious designation focuses on the analytical aspects of portfolio management. Three exams must be taken that cover financial-statement analysis, macro- and microeconomics, quantitative methods of investment analysis and management, financial markets and instruments, corporate finance, equity and fixed-income analysis, risk/return estimation, alternative investments, portfolio management including performance standards, and measurement techniques along with the AIMR code of ethics.

CHARTERED INVESTMENT COUNSELOR (CIC): GRANTED BY THE INVESTMENT COUNSELING ASSOCIATION OF AMERICA (ICAA)

Designated for experienced investment counselors and portfolio managers who already have the CFA.

PERSONAL FINANCIAL SPECIALIST (PFS): GRANTED BY THE AMERICAN INSTITUTE OF CERTIFIED PUBLIC ACCOUNTANTS (AICPA)

This designation is reserved for CPAs who also do financial planning. A 100-question exam must be passed, along with being a CPA and a member of the AICPA.

CERTIFIED PENSION CONSULTANT (CPC): GRANTED BY THE AMERICAN SOCIETY OF PENSION ACTUARIES (ASPA)

This is for advisors who work with employers to formulate, implement, administer, and maintain qualified retirement plans and other employee benefits.

CHARTERED RETIREMENT PLANS SPECIALIST (CRPS): GRANTED BY THE COLLEGE FOR FINANCIAL PLANNING

This designation is targeted to professionals who design, install, and administer retirement plans for businesses.

CHARTERED RETIREMENT PLANNING COUNSELOR (CRPC): GRANTED BY THE COLLEGE FOR FINANCIAL PLANNING

This designation is for advisors who do pre- and postretirement planning for individuals.

CERTIFIED RETIREMENT COUNSELOR (CRC): GRANTED BY THE INTERNATIONAL FOUNDATION FOR RETIREMENT EDUCATION

Designed for financial-services professionals who assist employees in making retirement-planning decisions.

Accredited Asset Manager Specialist (AAMS): Granted by The College for Financial Planning

Designed for advisors interested in specializing in asset management in a number of different areas, including investments, insurance, tax, retirement, and estate planning.

Board Certified in Asset Allocation (BCAA): Granted by The Institute of Business and Finance

A designation developed for advisors who deal with the general public as opposed to portfolio managers.

Board Certified in Securities (BCS): Granted by The Institute of Business and Finance

Designed for professionals interested in specializing in asset allocation.

Chartered Mutual Fund Counselor (CMFC): Granted by The College for Financial Planning

This designation is for advisors who are looking for comprehensive knowledge of mutual funds and how to use them.

Certified Funds Specialist (CFS): Granted by The Institute of Business and Finance

A certification aimed at comprehensive mutual fund analysis and strategy.

Certified Annuity Specialist (CAS): Granted by The Institute of Business and Finance

Designed for professionals who want advanced training in annuity strategies and their application.

Certified Senior Consultant (CSC): Granted by The Institute of Business and Finance

Designed for professionals interested in specializing in the issues facing investors over age fifty.

CERTIFIED SENIOR SPECIALIST (CSS): GRANTED BY THE CENTER FOR SENIOR STUDIES

Designed for the financial professional serving the fifty+ market.

CERTIFIED SENIOR ADVISOR (CSA): GRANTED BY THE SOCIETY OF CERTIFIED SENIOR ADVISORS

Designed for professionals who work with people over age sixty-five.

ACCREDITED ESTATE PLANNER (AEP): GRANTED BY THE NATIONAL ASSOCIATION OF ESTATE PLANNERS AND COUNCILS (NAEPC)

This designation is available to attorneys and advisors with the following designations: CPA, CLU, CFA, and CFP.

BOARD CERTIFIED IN ESTATE PLANNING (BCEP): GRANTED BY THE INSTITUTE OF BUSINESS AND FINANCE

Designed for brokers, advisors, and planners covering estate accumulation, preservation, and distribution.

ACCREDITED INVESTMENT FIDUCIARY (AIF): GRANTED BY THE CENTER OF FIDUCIARY STUDIES

This designation illustrates knowledge and competence in the area of fiduciary responsibility. AIF is for investment advisors, broker/dealers, and money managers.

ACCREDITED INVESTMENT FIDUCIARY AUDITOR (AIFA): GRANTED BY THE CENTER OF FIDUCIARY STUDIES

This designation illustrates knowledge and competence in the area of fiduciary responsibility. AIFA is for accountants, attorneys, and senior consultants who are in a position to audit an organization's investment process as it relates to fiduciary standards of care.

CERTIFIED COLLEGE PLANNING SPECIALIST (CCPS): GRANTED
BY THE NATIONAL INSTITUTE OF CERTIFIED COLLEGE
PLANNERS (NICCP)

Designed for financial advisors who actively assist families in preparing for the financial cost of sending children to college.

PROFESSIONAL ASSOCIATIONS

3 Dimensional Wealth International
Investment Management Consultants Association (IMCA)
Financial Planning Association (FPA)
International Association of Advisors in Philanthropy
Investment Counseling Association of America (ICAA)
Association for Investment Management and Research (AIMR)
American Institute of Certified Public Accountants (AICPA)
American Society of Pension Actuaries (ASPA)
The International Foundation for Retirement Education
The Institute for Business and Finance
The College for Financial Planning
The Center for Senior Studies
The Society of Certified Senior Advisors
The National Association of Estate Planners and Councils (NAEPC)
The Center of Fiduciary Studies
The National Institute of Certified College Planners (NICCP)

SUGGESTED READING

BOOKS

PERSONAL WEALTH

Brooks, Robert and Sam Goldstein. *Raising Resilient Children: Fostering Strength, Hope and Optimism in Your Child.* Lincolnwood, IL: Contemporary Books, 2001.

Buford, Bob. *Game Plan.* Grand Rapids, MI: Zondervan Press, 1997.

Buford, Bob. *Half Time.* Grand Rapids, MI: Zondervan Press, 1994.

Covey, Stephen. *Seven Habits of Highly Effective Families.* New York: Simon & Schuster, 1989.

Hughes, Jr., James E. *Family Wealth: Keeping It in the Family.* Princeton, NJ: Bloomberg Press, 2004.

Maxwell, John C. *Failing Forward.* Nashville, TN: Thomas Nelson Publishers, 2000.

McCarthy, Kevin. *The On-Purpose Person.* Colorado Springs, CO: Pinion Press, 1992.

Morley, Patrick. *Man in the Mirror.* Grand Rapids, MI: Zondervan Press, 1989.

Willis, Thayer. *Navigating the Dark Side of Wealth.* Zanesville, OH: New Concord Press, 2003.

Financial Wealth

Bachrach, Bill. *Values Based Financial Planning.* Aim High Press, 2000.

Esperti, Peterson, Diefendorf. *Wealth: Enhancement & Preservation.* Denver, CO: The Institute, 1995.

Esperti, Peterson, Diefendorf, Madden. *21st Century Wealth.* Denver, CO: Quantum Press, 2000.

Link, E.G. "Jay." *Getting to the Heart of the Matter.* Professional Mentoring Program, 1999.

Social Wealth

Block, Peter. *Stewardship.* San Francisco: Berrett-Koehler Publishers, 1993.

Hillman, Os. *Today God Is First.* Destiny Image Publishers, 2000.

Smith, Hyrum W. *What Matters Most: The Power of Living Your Values.*

Stovall, Jim. *The Ultimate Gift.* Mechanicsburg, PA: Executive Books, 1999.

Williams, Roy & Vic Preisser. *Philanthropy: Heirs & Values.* Robert D. Reed Publishing, 2005.

Websites

Personal Wealth

www.FamilyLegacyManuscript.com (The Foundation for the Preservation and Encouragement of Family Values)

www.injoy.com (The INJOY Group)
www.maninthemirror.com (Man in the Mirror)
www.focusonthefamily.com (Focus on the Family)

Financial Wealth

www.DiefendorfCapital.com (Diefendorf Capital Planning Associates)
www.learntosave.com (Learn to Save)
www.youngbiz.com/drivingyourfuture/ (Driving Your Future)
www.maddenfin.com (Madden Financial Services)
www.CPRvia.com (Consolidated Portfolio Review Corp)
www.SterlingMonroe.com (Sterling Monroe Securities)
www.RPAtpa.com (Retirement Planning and Administration)
www.TheTaxAdvisoryGroup.com (The Tax Advisory Group)
www.Dief-Insure.com (Diefendorf Planning Services)
www.makingallowances.com (Making Allowances)
www.publicdebt.treas.gov/mar/marmoneymath.htm (Money Math)
www.prosperity4kids.com (Prosperity 4 Kids)
www.SCDria.com (Structured Capital Designs, Inc.)
www.strongkids.com (Strong Kids)
www.wisepockets.com (Wise Pockets)
www.practicalmoneyskills.com (Practical Money Skills)
www.101financiallessons.com (101 Financial Lessons)
www.aarp.org/life (AARP)
www.aoa.dhhs.gov (Administration on Aging)
www.careguide.com (Careguide.com)
www.nolo.com (Nolo.com)
www.parentcaresolution.com/main.html (The Parent Care Solution)

Social Wealth

www.FoundationSource.com (Private Foundation Administration)
www.foundationforfamilyvalues.com (The Foundation for the Encouragement & Preservation of Family Values)

About the Authors

Monroe "Roey" M. Diefendorf, Jr., MI, CLU, ChFC, CFP, RFC, CIMA, C3DWP

152 Forest Ave., Locust Valley, NY 11560 * 516-759-3900

Active since 1970, Roey is the fourth generation of his family in the business and is currently the CEO of Diefendorf Capital Planning Associates.

Following his graduation from Deerfield Academy and Bucknell University with a degree in behavioral psychology, Roey earned a master's degree in insurance from Georgia State University, with a major in estate planning and a minor in pension planning. In 1976 and 1983, he received the designations of chartered life underwriter (CLU) and chartered financial consultant (ChFC), from the American College, Bryn Mawr, Pennsylvania. In 1992, he was designated a certified financial planner (CFP) by the College of Financial Planners in Denver, Colorado. In addition, Roey has been admitted as a CFP practitioner. In March 2001, he was designated registered financial consultant (RFC). In 2003, he attended the Wharton School of Business at the University of Pennsylvania and successfully completed the certified investment management analyst (CIMA) designation. As an industry leader, Roey has coauthored the books *Wealth: Enhancement & Preservation* (1995) and *21st Century Wealth* (2000). Over the years he has been a speaker at several international industry conferences and has made several guest appearances on the Cable TV program *Dollars & Sense*. In January of 2003, Roey was interviewed by Forbes Radio. The interview aired on over 192,000 flights on American Airlines. His passion is consulting in the areas of family wealth counseling and philanthropic estate planning. He is a charter member of The International Association of Advisors in Philanthropy. In 2001, Roey's registered investment advisory firm, Consolidated Portfolio Review Corp., was recognized for its significant revenue growth and was one of ten recipients nationwide to receive the Fleet Bank Small Business Leadership Award, recognized for its significant revenue growth. In 2002, he created The Foundation for the Encouragement & Preservation of Family Values, LLC, which is a member of the Association of Personal Historians (APH). As CEO, Roey is a member of the Fellowship of Companies for Christ International (FCCI). He has served on the boards of LI Young Life and Daystar University, Athi River, Kenya, East Africa. Roey and his wife Chris founded Hope for Long Island and the North Shore Community Church, PCA in Oyster Bay, New York and Roey is a Ruling Elder. In addition, Roey is the founder and registered principal of Sterling Monroe Securities, LLC, member NASD, SIPC, and a member of the Investment Management Consultants Association (IMCA) and the National Association of Independent Broker Dealers (NAIBD). Finally, Roey oversees the Diefendorf family of financial service companies, which include, Consolidated Portfolio Review Corp., Diefendorf Planning Services, Ltd., Retirement Planning & Administration, Inc., Sterling Monroe Securities, LLC, Structured Capital Designs, Inc., and The Tax Advisory Group, LLC. In 2004, Roey opened his first virtual office in Pinehurst, North Carolina with the establishment of 3 Dimensional Wealth Counseling of North Carolina. In addition, he is the founder of 3 Dimensional Wealth International, an association for values-based advisors that issues the professional designation Certified 3 Dimensional Wealth Practitioner (C3DWP). You can hear Roey each Monday, 5:00–6:00 p.m. EST, on his syndicated Internet radio show *3 Dimensional Wealth* at www.Business. VoiceAmerica.com. He resides in Laurel Hollow, New York, with Chris and four daughters, Ashley, Jennie Monroe, Whitney, and Emily.

www.DiefendorfCapital.com

ROBERT S. MADDEN, CLU, ChFC, CFP

1000 Woodbury Road, Suite 400 Woodbury, NY 11797 * 516-682-3429

Bob graduated from the United States Naval Academy in 1972. He served first as a Surface Warfare Officer and later as an instructor of leadership at Naval Officer Candidate School, Newport, Rhode Island. He continues to represent the Naval Academy as a Blue and Gold officer for his native Long Island area, interviewing and assisting young men and women candidates desiring appointment. Bob earned a master's in education (counseling) from Providence College in 1978, and in 1983 he completed an MBA at the New York Institute of Technology. After leaving the naval service, Bob helped run his family business for a short time prior to taking a position in business/program management at Hazeltine Corporation, a defense electronics company. He was responsible for the successful design and delivery of critical components of several military programs, including Patriot Air Defense System, DIVAD, and the B-2 Stealth Bomber. While at Hazeltine, Bob started an investment club for fellow employees interested in implementing their financial goals. Bob entered the financial services industry on a full-time basis in 1986. He is currently a registered principal as well as a registered representative and investment adviser representative of MML Investor Services, Inc. In addition to his individual practice, Bob serves in the capacity of investment specialist as well as director of fee-based financial planning for the Island Financial Group in Woodbury, New York. He provides fee-based financial plans, investment and insurance solutions, and corporate and small-business benefit plans. Bob focuses on developing and implementing long-term financial strategies based on his clients' unique goals and objectives. Bob is often a featured speaker at financial workshops that focus on wealth accumulation, protection planning, retirement planning, and estate conservation. He continues to chair numerous committees in the business environment and in his community. He was a contributing author to the book *21ˢᵗ Century Wealth* (2000). Bob is a deacon/trustee and treasurer of his church and is the chairman of the building committee for Operation Lighthouse. He has three children: Rob, Alie, and Mike; daughter-in-law Cheri; and three grandchildren: Victoria,

Alex, and Ashton. He and his wife Cindy live in Huntington, New York. They are involved in numerous charitable organizations.

My 3 Dimensional Wealth Plan

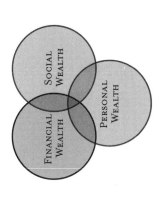

FINANCIAL WEALTH • SOCIAL WEALTH • PERSONAL WEALTH

_____ YEAR

FOLD

PARADIGMS

1. Inwardly focused is out.
   Outwardly focused is in.

2. Balance sheet accounting is out
   Balanced life accounting is in.

3. Spend, save, then give is out.
   Give, save, then spend is in.

4. Instant gratification is out.
   Future gratification is in.

5. Ownership is out.
   Stewardship is in.

6. One-dimensional wealth is out.
   3 Dimensional Wealth is in.

The health of your family's wealth must be measured in terms that cannot be quantified in dollars alone. *3 Dimensional Wealth* takes your family through this process, which combines tradition, values, and monetary solutions for generations to come.

FOLD

SUGGESTIONS

1. Carry with you and refer to frequently.

2. Cross out each goal as it is achieved.

3. Do not make goals unrealistic so as to be unmeaningful because they are beyond achievement.

4. To commit yourself to goals is the first step to a worthwhile life.

5. To attain the goals you set is the true fulfillment of your life's purpose.

6. Review your 3 Dimensional Wealth balance ratios.

MAKE THIS THE BEST YEAR FOR YOU AND YOUR FAMILY!

MY CORE VALUES ARE:

PERSONAL WEALTH

PILLARS OF IMPORTANCE:

1.
2.
3.
4.
5.

GOALS:

1.
2.
3.
4.
5.

My Personal Wealth Purpose Statement:

My Personal Wealth Vision Statement:

My Personal Wealth Mission Statement:

FOLD

FINANCIAL WEALTH

PILLARS OF IMPORTANCE:

1.
2.
3.
4.
5.

GOALS:

1.
2.
3.
4.
5.

My Financial Wealth Purpose Statement:

My Financial Wealth Vision Statement:

My Financial Wealth Mission Statement:

FOLD

SOCIAL WEALTH

PILLARS OF IMPORTANCE:

1.
2.
3.
4.
5.

GOALS:

1.
2.
3.
4.
5.

My Social Wealth Purpose Statement:

My Social Wealth Vision Statement:

My Social Wealth Mission Statement: